MATH Trailblazers®

A BALANCED MATHEMATICS PROGRAM INTEGRATING SCIENCE AND LANGUAGE ARTS

Facts Resource Guide

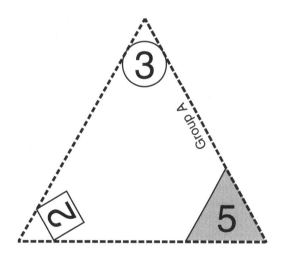

THIRD EDITION

KENDALL/HUNT PUBLISHING COMPANY
4050 Westmark Drive   Dubuque, Iowa 52002

A TIMS® Curriculum
University of Illinois at Chicago

UIC The University of Illinois
at Chicago

The original edition was based on work supported by the National Science Foundation under grant No. MDR 9050226 and the University of Illinois at Chicago. Any opinions, findings, and conclusions or recommendations expressed in this publication are those of the author(s) and do not necessarily reflect the views of the granting agencies.

Grade 2 Acknowledgments

Teaching Integrated Mathematics and Science (TIMS) Project Directors

Philip Wagreich, Principal Investigator

Joan L. Bieler

Howard Goldberg (emeritus)

Catherine Randall Kelso

Director

Third Edition   Joan L. Bieler

Curriculum Developers

Third Edition   Lindy M. Chambers-Boucher   Philip Wagreich

Janet Simpson Beissinger

Contributors

Third Edition

Eileen Wynn Ball	Sandy Niemiera
Jenny Bay-Williams	Christina Nugent
Ava Chatterjee-Belisle	Janet M. Parsons
Elizabeth Colligan	Leona Peters
Marty Gartzman	Catherine Reed
Carol Inzerillo	

Editorial and Production Staff

Third Edition

Kathleen R. Anderson	Christina Clemons
Lindy M. Chambers-Boucher	Anne Roby

TIMS Professional Developers

Barbara Crum	Cheryl Kneubuhler
Catherine Ditto	Lisa Mackey
Pamela Guyton	Linda Miceli

TIMS Director of Media Services

Henrique Cirne-Lima

TIMS Research Staff

Stacy Brown	Catherine Ditto
Reality Canty	Kathleen Pitvorec
Alison Castro	Catherine Randall Kelso

TIMS Administrative Staff

Eve Ali Boles	Enrique Puente
Kathleen R. Anderson	Alice VanSlyke
Nida Khan	

Director

Second Edition   Catherine Randall Kelso

Curriculum Developers

Second Edition

Lindy M. Chambers-Boucher
Elizabeth Colligan
Marty Gartzman
Carol Inzerillo
Catherine Randall Kelso

Jennifer Mundt Leimberer
Georganne E. Marsh
Leona Peters
Philip Wagreich

Editorial and Production Staff

Second Edition

Kathleen R. Anderson
Ai-Ai C. Cojuangco
Andrada Costoiu
Erika Larsen

Georganne E. Marsh
Cosmina Menghes
Anne Roby

Principal Investigators

First Edition

Philip Wagreich

Howard Goldberg

Senior Curriculum Developers

First Edition

Janet Simpson Beissinger
Joan L. Bieler
Astrida Cirulis
Marty Gartzman
Howard Goldberg

Carol Inzerillo
Andy Isaacs
Catherine Randall Kelso
Leona Peters
Philip Wagreich

Curriculum Developers

First Edition

Janice C. Banasiak
Lynne Beauprez
Andy Carter
Lindy M. Chambers-Boucher
Kathryn Chval
Diane Czerwinski

Jenny Knight
Sandy Niemiera
Janice Ozima
Polly Tangora
Paul Trafton

Illustrator

First Edition

Kris Dresen

Editorial and Production Staff

First Edition

Glenda L. Genio-Terrado
Mini Joseph
Lynette Morgenthaler

Sarah Nelson
Birute Petrauskas
Anne Roby

Research Consultant

First Edition

Andy Isaacs

Mathematics Education Consultant

First Edition

Paul Trafton

National Advisory Committee

First Edition

Carl Berger
Tom Berger
Hugh Burkhart
Donald Chambers
Naomi Fisher
Glenda Lappan

Mary Lindquist
Eugene Maier
Lourdes Monteagudo
Elizabeth Phillips
Thomas Post

Grade 2 Table of Contents

Math Trailblazers® includes a comprehensive, research-based program for teaching basic math facts. This program is carefully integrated into the lessons and Daily Practice and Problems (DPP) of each grade and the Home Practice in Grades 3–5. The *Grade 2 Facts Resource Guide* is a compilation of much of the math facts materials for second grade. These include math facts lessons, relevant DPP items, flash cards, the TIMS Tutor: *Math Facts,* and information for parents about *Math Trailblazers* math facts philosophy.

Classrooms that stay close to the suggested pacing schedule for teaching lessons will have little difficulty implementing the complete math facts program without the use of this guide. In those classrooms, teachers can simply use the math facts materials built into the lessons and Daily Practice and Problems. However, because the math facts program is closely linked to the recommended schedule for teaching, classrooms that differ significantly from the suggested pacing will need to make special accommodations to ensure that students receive a consistent program of math facts practice and assessment throughout the year. This manual will assist teachers with that process. A pacing schedule is in the Grade 2 Overview section in the *Teacher Implementation Guide.*

All materials included in the *Grade 2 Facts Resource Guide* are located elsewhere in *Math Trailblazers.* Wherever appropriate, we will include a reference to an item's location in other *Math Trailblazers* components.

What Is the Math Trailblazers Facts Resource Guide?

A major goal of *Math Trailblazers* is to prepare students to compute accurately, flexibly, and appropriately in all situations. Standard topics in arithmetic—acquisition of basic math facts and fluency with whole-number operations—are covered extensively.

In developing our program for the math facts, we sought a careful balance between strategies and drill. This approach is based on a large body of research and advocated by the National Council of Teachers of Mathematics (NCTM) *Principles and Standards for School Mathematics* and by the National Research Council in *Adding It Up: Helping Children Learn Mathematics.* The research indicates that the methods used in the *Math Trailblazers* math facts program lead to more effective learning and better retention of the math facts and also help develop essential math skills.

For a detailed discussion of the math facts program in *Math Trailblazers,* see Section 3 TIMS Tutor: *Math Facts.* See also Section 2 *Information for Parents: Math Facts Philosophy.*

Introduction to the Math Facts in Math Trailblazers

The following table describes the development of math facts and whole number operations in *Math Trailblazers*. The shaded portions of the table highlight development of the math facts program in each grade. Expectations for fluency with math facts are indicated in bold. The white portions of the table highlight development of the whole-number operations.

Grade	Addition	Subtraction	Multiplication	Division
K	Introduce concepts through problem solving and use of manipulatives.			
1	Develop strategies for addition facts. Solve addition problems in context.	Develop strategies for subtraction facts. Solve subtraction problems in context.	Develop concepts through problem solving and use of manipulatives.	
2	Continue use of addition facts in problems. Continue use of strategies for addition facts. **Assess for fluency with addition facts.** Continue solving addition problems in context. Introduce procedures for multidigit addition using manipulatives and paper and pencil.	Continue use of subtraction facts in problems. Continue use of strategies for subtraction facts. **Assess for fluency with subtraction facts.** Continue solving subtraction problems in context. Introduce procedures for multidigit subtraction using manipulatives and paper and pencil.	Continue concept development through problem solving and use of manipulatives.	
3	Diagnose and remediate with addition facts as needed. Develop procedures for multidigit addition using manipulatives and paper and pencil. Practice and apply multidigit addition in varied contexts.	Maintain fluency with subtraction facts through review and assessment. Develop procedures for multidigit subtraction using manipulatives and paper and pencil. Practice and apply multidigit subtraction in varied contexts.	Continue use of multiplication facts in problems. Develop strategies for multiplication facts. **Assess for fluency with multiplication facts.** Solve multiplication problems in context. Introduce paper-and-pencil multiplication of one digit by two digits.	Continue use of division facts in problems. Develop strategies for division facts. Continue concept development. Solve division problems in context.
4	Diagnose and remediate with addition facts as needed. Practice and apply multidigit addition in varied contexts. Review paper-and-pencil procedures for multidigit addition.	Diagnose and remediate with subtraction facts as needed. Practice and apply multidigit subtraction in varied contexts. Review paper-and-pencil procedures for multidigit subtraction.	Maintain fluency with multiplication facts through review and assessment. Develop procedures for multiplication using manipulatives and paper and pencil (1-digit and 2-digit multipliers). Practice and apply multiplication in varied contexts.	Continue use of division facts in problems. Continue development of strategies for division facts. **Assess for fluency with division facts.** Solve division problems in context. Develop procedures for division using manipulatives and paper and pencil (1-digit divisors).
5	Diagnose and remediate with addition facts as needed. Practice and apply multidigit addition in varied contexts.	Diagnose and remediate with subtraction facts as needed. Practice and apply multidigit subtraction in varied contexts.	Maintain fluency with multiplication facts through review and assessment. Review paper-and-pencil procedures. Practice and apply multiplication in varied contexts.	Maintain fluency with division facts through review and assessment. Develop paper-and-pencil procedures with one- and two-digit divisors. Practice and apply division in varied contexts.

Table 1: *Math Facts and Whole-Number Operations Overview*

Addition and Subtraction Practice and Assessment

A yearlong, systematic, strategies-based review of the addition facts begins in Unit 3. Students review and are assessed on the addition facts in small groups as outlined below in Table 2. In Units 11–20, students concentrate on the subtraction facts. For a detailed explanation of our approach to learning and assessing the facts, see the TIMS Tutor: *Math Facts* in Section 3 of this book or in the *Teacher Implementation Guide*.

Unit	Review and Assessment of the Math Facts Groups
1	Review
2	Review
3	Review the addition facts in Group A (0 + 1, 1 + 1, 2 + 1, 3 + 1, 0 + 2, 2 + 2, 3 + 2, 4 + 2) Quiz on the addition facts in Group A
4	Review the addition facts in Group B (3 + 0, 4 + 0, 5 + 0, 4 + 1, 5 + 1, 6 + 1, 5 + 2, 6 + 2, 5 + 3) Quiz on the addition facts in Group B
5	Review the addition facts in Group C (3 + 3, 3 + 4, 4 + 4, 4 + 5, 5 + 5, 5 + 6, 5 + 7, 6 + 6) Quiz on the addition facts in Group C
6	Review the addition facts in Group D (1 + 7, 2 + 7, 1 + 8, 2 + 8, 3 + 6, 3 + 7, 3 + 8, 4 + 6, 4 + 7, 4 + 8) Quiz on the addition facts in Group D
7	Review the addition facts in Group E (6 + 7, 7 + 7, 7 + 8, 5 + 8, 6 + 8, 8 + 8, 9 + 9, 9 + 10) Quiz on the addition facts in Group E
8	Review the addition facts in Group F (9 + 1, 9 + 2, 9 + 3, 9 + 4, 10 + 1, 10 + 2, 10 + 3, 10 + 4) Quiz on the addition facts in Group F
9	Review the addition facts in Group G (9 + 5, 9 + 6, 9 + 7, 9 + 8, 10 + 5, 10 + 6, 10 + 7, 10 + 8) Quiz on the addition facts in Group G
10	Review and assess the addition facts in Groups A–G Inventory Test on the addition facts in Groups A–G
11	Review the subtraction facts for Group A (1 − 1, 1 − 0, 2 − 1, 3 − 2, 3 − 1, 4 − 3, 4 − 1, 2 − 2, 2 − 0, 4 − 2, 5 − 3, 5 − 2, 6 − 4, 6 − 2) Quiz on the subtraction facts for Group A
12	Review the subtraction facts for Group B (3 − 0, 3 − 3, 4 − 0, 4 − 4, 5 − 0, 5 − 5, 5 − 1, 5 − 4, 6 − 5, 6 − 1, 7 − 6, 7 − 1, 7 − 5, 7 − 2, 8 − 6, 8 − 2, 8 − 5, 8 − 3) Quiz on the subtraction facts for Group B
13	Review the subtraction facts for Group C (6 − 3, 7 − 3, 7 − 4, 8 − 4, 9 − 4, 9 − 5, 10 − 5, 11 − 5, 11 − 6, 12 − 5, 12 − 7, 12 − 6) Quiz on the subtraction facts for Group C
14	Review the subtraction facts for Group D (8 − 1, 8 − 7, 9 − 1, 9 − 8, 9 − 2, 9 − 7, 10 − 2, 10 − 8, 9 − 3, 9 − 6, 10 − 3, 10 − 7, 11 − 3, 11 − 8, 10 − 4, 10 − 6, 11 − 4, 11 − 7, 12 − 4, 12 − 8) Quiz on the subtraction facts for Group D

(continued next page)

Table 2: *Math Facts Groups*

Unit	Review and Assessment of the Math Facts Groups *(continued)*
15	Review the subtraction facts for Group E (13 − 7, 13 − 6, 14 − 7, 15 − 7, 15 − 8, 13 − 5, 13 − 8, 14 − 6, 14 − 8, 16 − 8, 18 − 9, 19 − 9, 19 − 10) Quiz on the subtraction facts for Group E
16	Review the subtraction facts for Group F (10 − 1, 10 − 9, 11 − 2, 11 − 9, 12 − 3, 12 − 9, 13 − 4, 13 − 9, 11 − 1, 11 − 10, 12 − 2, 12 − 10, 13 − 3, 13 − 10, 14 − 4, 14 − 10) Quiz on the subtraction facts for Group F
17	Review the subtraction facts for Group G (14 − 5, 14 − 9, 15 − 9, 15 − 6, 16 − 9, 16 − 7, 17 − 8, 17 − 9, 15 − 5, 15 − 10, 16 − 10, 16 − 6, 17 − 10, 17 – 7, 18 − 10, 18 − 8) Quiz on the subtraction facts for Group G
18	Review and assess the addition and subtraction facts for Groups A–D
19	Review and assess the addition and subtraction facts for Groups E–G
20	Review and assess the addition and subtraction facts for Groups A–G Inventory Test on the addition and subtraction facts for Groups A–G

(continued from previous page)

Table 2: *Math Facts Groups*

Launching the Study of the Addition and Subtraction Facts. In Units 3–10, students first assess their fluency with the addition facts using *Triangle Flash Cards.* Unit 3 Lesson 4 *Addition with Triangle Flash Cards* begins the addition math facts strand in Grade 2. Students learn to use the *Triangle Flash Cards* to study the addition facts.

After completing Lesson 4, students continue to practice the addition facts in Group A by completing DPP items. Near the end of the unit, a DPP item includes a quiz on the addition facts for Group A. Students use a similar process in Units 4–10 to study the addition facts in Groups B–G.

In Units 11–20, students study the subtraction facts using the same process. Unit 11 Lesson 1 *Subtraction with Triangle Flash Cards* begins the subtraction math facts strand in Grade 2. Students learn to use the *Triangle Flash Cards* to study the subtraction facts. Students also explore fact families.

Sorting Triangle Flash Cards. When each fact group is introduced in the DPP, students practice their facts with a partner using *Triangle Flash Cards.* Students sort the cards into three piles: those they know and can answer quickly, those they can figure out with a strategy, and those they need to learn. After sorting the flash cards, students discuss the strategies they used to find the answers.

Distributed Facts Practice. Practice of each group of facts is distributed throughout the DPP in each unit: the addition facts in Units 3–10, the subtraction facts in Units 11–17, and both the addition and subtraction facts in Units 18–20.

Quizzes and Inventory Tests. To assess students on each group of facts, short quizzes are offered regularly in the DPP. The short quizzes are less threatening to students and are as effective as longer tests, so we strongly recommend against weekly testing of 60 to 100 facts. Unit 10 includes an inventory test for the addition facts while Unit 20 includes an inventory test for the addition and subtraction facts.

As indicated, the *Math Trailblazers* program for teaching math facts in Grade 2 is based on a distributed study of the facts, located largely in the DPP for each unit. The orderly distribution of the facts will be disrupted if the pacing of the program is altered from the recommended schedule. The *Grade 2 Facts Resource Guide* provides an alternative schedule for the study and assessment of math facts for teachers who fall significantly behind the estimated number of class sessions assigned per unit. (If you do not fall behind the recommended schedule, you do not need the *Grade 2 Facts Resource Guide*—simply follow the math facts program in the units.)

The *Grade 2 Facts Resource Guide* translates the math facts program into a week-by-week calendar that roughly approximates the schedule for studying the math facts that a class would follow if they remain close to the designated schedule for *Math Trailblazers* lessons. (See the Math Facts Calendar in Section 4.) In this manner, students will review all the math facts for their particular grade even if they do not complete all the units for the year.

This program is based on research that shows that students learn the facts better using a strategies-based approach accompanied by distributed practice of small groups of facts. Therefore, we strongly recommend against using the math facts program in a shorter amount of time. Those students who know the facts based on the *Triangle Flash Cards* self-assessment will not need much practice. Other students will find they only need to study one or two facts in a group. Still others will need to work on more facts, using the flash cards and games at home.

It is important to note that in *Math Trailblazers* much of the work for gaining fluency with math facts arises naturally in the problem-solving activities completed in class and in the homework. Thus, the math facts items included in the *Grade 2 Facts Resource Guide* do not reflect the full scope of the math facts program in the *Math Trailblazers* curriculum.

Using the *Facts Resource Guide*

Resources

Fuson, K.C. "Developing Mathematical Power in Whole Number Operations." In *A Research Companion to Principles and Standards for School Mathematics*. National Council of Teachers of Mathematics, Reston, VA, 2003.

Isaacs, A.C., and W.M. Carroll. "Strategies for Basic Facts Instruction." *Teaching Children Mathematics,* 5 May, pp 508–15, 1999.

National Research Council. "Developing Proficiency with Whole Numbers." In *Adding It Up: Helping Children Learn Mathematics,* J. Kilpatrick, J. Swafford, and B. Findell, eds. National Academy Press, Washington, DC, 2001.

Principles and Standards for School Mathematics. National Council of Teachers of Mathematics, Reston, VA, 2000.

Thornton, C.A. "Strategies for the Basic Facts." In J.N. Payne (ed.), *Mathematics for the Young Child.* National Council of Teachers of Mathematics, Reston, VA, 1990.

To inform parents about the curriculum's goals and philosophy of learning and assessing the math facts, send home a copy of the *Grade 2 Math Facts Philosophy* that immediately follows. This document is also available in the Unit 3 *Unit Resource Guide* immediately following the Background and on the *Teacher Resource CD*.

Information for Parents

Grade 2 Math Facts Philosophy

The goal of the math facts strand in *Math Trailblazers* is for students to learn the basic facts efficiently, to gain fluency with their use, and to retain that fluency over time. In second grade, students are expected to demonstrate fluency with the addition and subtraction facts.

A large body of research supports an approach in which students develop strategies for figuring out the facts rather than relying on rote memorization. This not only leads to more effective learning and better retention, but also to the development of mental math skills. In fact, too much drill before conceptual understanding may actually interfere with a child's ability to understand concepts at a later date. Therefore, the teaching of the basic facts in *Math Trailblazers* is characterized by the following elements:

- **Use of Strategies.** In all grades we encourage the use of strategies to find facts, so students become confident that they can find answers to fact problems that they do not immediately recall. In this way, students learn that math is more than memorizing facts and rules that "you either get or you don't."

- **Distributed Facts Practice.** Students study small groups of facts that can be found using similar strategies. In second grade, they focus on the addition facts in the first semester and the subtraction facts in the second semester. Students use *Triangle Flash Cards* to study each group of facts at home.

- **Practice in Context.** Students continue to practice all the facts as they use them to solve problems in labs, activities, and games.

- **Appropriate Assessment.** Students' progress with the math facts is assessed as they complete activities, labs, and games. Students take quizzes on each group of facts as they study them. Students must solve fact problems and describe their strategies. Students also take an inventory test of all the addition facts at the end of the first semester and the addition and subtraction facts at the end of the second semester.

- **Facts Will Not Act as Gatekeepers.** Use of strategies and calculators allows students to continue to work on interesting problems and experiments while they are learning the facts. Students are not prevented from learning more complex mathematics because they do not have quick recall of the facts.

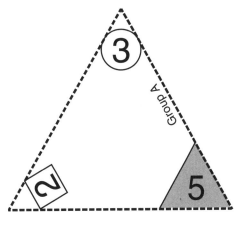

A sample *Triangle Flash Card*

Información para los padres

La filosofía de los conceptos matemáticos básicos en 2do grado

El objetivo de la enseñanza de los conceptos matemáticos en *Math Trailblazers* es que los estudiantes aprendan los conceptos básicos eficazmente, logren el dominio del uso de estos conceptos y mantengan ese dominio con el paso del tiempo. En segundo grado, se espera que los estudiantes demuestren tener dominio de las sumas y restas básicas.

Las extensas investigaciones realizadas respaldan la aplicación de un enfoque en el que los estudiantes desarrollan estrategias para resolver las operaciones en lugar de hacerlo de memoria. Esto no sólo permite un aprendizaje más eficaz y una mejor retención, sino que también promueve el desarrollo de habilidades matemáticas mentales. De hecho, el exceso de repetición antes de comprender los conceptos puede interferir con la habilidad de los niños para entender conceptos más adelante. Por lo tanto, la enseñanza y la evaluación de los conceptos básicos en *Math Trailblazers* se caracterizan por los siguientes elementos:

El uso de estrategias. En todos los grados, alentamos el uso de estrategias para resolver operaciones básicas, de modo que los estudiantes tengan la confianza de que pueden hallar soluciones a problemas que no recuerdan inmediatamente. De esta manera, los estudiantes aprenden que las matemáticas son más que tablas y reglas memorizadas que un estudiante "sabe o no sabe".

Práctica gradual de los conceptos básicos. Los estudiantes estudian pequeños grupos de conceptos básicos que pueden hallarse usando estrategias similares. En segundo grado, se concentran en las sumas básicas durante el primer semestre y en las restas básicas durante el segundo semestre. Los estudiantes usan tarjetas triangulares en casa para estudiar cada grupo de conceptos básicos en casa.

Práctica en contexto. Los estudiantes continúan practicando todos los conceptos básicos a medida que los usan para resolver problemas en las investigaciones, las actividades y los juegos.

Evaluación apropiada. El progreso de los estudiantes con las sumas básicas también se evalúa a medida que completan actividades, experimentos y juegos. Los estudiantes también toman exámenes sobre cada grupo de conceptos básicos a medida que los estudian. Los estudiantes deben resolver problemas de suma y resta y describir sus estrategias. Los estudiantes también tomarán un examen acerca de todas las sumas básicas al final del primer semestre y acerca de las sumas y restas básicas al final del segundo semestre.

El nivel de dominio de los conceptos básicos no impedirá el aprendizaje. El uso de estrategias y calculadoras permite a los estudiantes continuar trabajando con problemas y experimentos interesantes mientras aprenden los conceptos básicos. Si los estudiantes no recuerdan fácilmente los conceptos básicos, podrán igualmente aprender conceptos matemáticos más complejos.

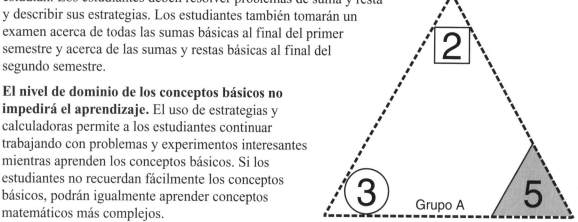

Un ejemplo de una tarjeta triangular

The TIMS Tutor: *Math Facts* provides an in-depth exploration of the math facts concepts and ideas behind the math facts strand in *Math Trailblazers*. This document also appears in the *Teacher Implementation Guide*.

Students need to learn the math facts. Estimation, mental arithmetic, checking the reasonableness of results, and paper-and-pencil calculations require the ability to give quick, accurate responses when using basic facts. The question is not if students should learn the math facts, but how. Which teaching methods are most efficient and effective? To answer this question, we as authors of *Math Trailblazers* drew upon educational research and our own classroom experiences to develop a comprehensive plan for teaching the math facts.

Philosophy

The goal of the *Math Trailblazers* math facts strand is for students to learn the basic facts efficiently, gain fluency with their use, and retain that fluency over time. A large body of research supports an approach that is built on a foundation of work with strategies and concepts. This not only leads to more effective learning and better retention, but also to development of mental math skills. Therefore, the teaching and assessment of the basic facts in *Math Trailblazers* is characterized by the following elements:

- *Early emphasis on problem solving.* Students first approach the basic facts as problems to solve rather than as facts to memorize. Students invent their own strategies to solve these problems or learn appropriate strategies from others through class discussion. Students' natural strategies, especially counting strategies, are explicitly encouraged. In this way, students learn that math is more than memorizing facts and rules that "you either get or you don't."

- *De-emphasis of rote work.* Fluency with the math facts is an important component of any student's mathematical learning. Research shows that overemphasizing memorization and frequent administration of timed tests are counterproductive. Both can produce undesirable results (Isaacs and Carroll, 1999; Van de Walle, 2001; National Research Council, 2001). We encourage the use of strategies to find facts, so students become confident they can find answers to fact problems they do not immediately recall.

- *Gradual and systematic introduction of facts.* Students study the facts in small groups they solve using similar strategies. Students first work on simple strategies for easy facts and then progress to more sophisticated strategies and harder facts. By the end of the process, they gain fluency with all required facts.

- *Ongoing practice.* Work on the math facts is distributed throughout the curriculum, especially in the Daily Practice and Problems (DPP), Home Practice, and games. This practice for fluency, however, takes place only after students have a conceptual understanding of the operations and have achieved proficiency with strategies for solving basic fact problems. Delaying practice in this way means that less practice is required to achieve fluency.

- *Appropriate assessment.* Teachers assess students' knowledge of the facts through observations as they work on activities, labs, and games as well as through the appropriate use of written tests and quizzes. Beginning in first grade, periodic, short quizzes in the DPP naturally follow the study of small groups of facts organized around specific strategies. As self-assessment in Grades 3–5, students record their progress on *Facts I Know* charts and determine which facts they need to study. Inventory tests of all facts for each operation are used sparingly in Grades 2–5 (no more than twice per year) to assess students' progress with fact fluency. The goal of the math facts assessment program is to determine the degree to which students can find answers to fact problems quickly and accurately and whether they can retain this skill over time.
- *Multiyear approach.* In Grades 1 and 2, *Math Trailblazers* emphasizes strategies that lead to fluency with the addition and subtraction facts. In Grade 3, students gain fluency with the multiplication facts while reviewing the addition and subtraction facts. In Grade 4, students achieve fluency with the division facts and verify fluency with the multiplication facts. In Grade 5, the multiplication and division facts are systematically reviewed and assessed.
- *Facts are not gatekeepers.* Students are not prevented from learning more complex mathematics because they do not perform well on fact tests. Use of strategies, calculators, and other math tools (e.g., manipulatives, hundred charts, printed multiplication tables) allows students to continue to work on interesting problems while still learning the facts.

Expectations by Grade Level

The following goals for the math facts are consistent with the recommendations in the National Council of Teachers of Mathematics *Principles and Standards for School Mathematics:*

- In kindergarten, students use manipulatives and invent their own strategies to solve addition and subtraction problems.
- By the end of first grade, all students can solve all basic addition and subtraction problems using some strategy. Fluency is not emphasized; strategies are. Some work with beginning concepts of multiplication takes place.
- In second grade, learning efficient strategies for addition and especially subtraction continues to be emphasized. Work with multiplication concepts continues. By the end of the year, students are expected to demonstrate fluency with all the addition and subtraction facts.
- In third grade, students review the subtraction facts. They develop efficient strategies for learning the multiplication facts and demonstrate fluency with the multiplication facts.
- In fourth grade, students review the multiplication facts and develop strategies for the division facts. By the end of year, we expect fluency with all the division facts.
- In fifth grade, students review the multiplication and division facts and are expected to maintain fluency with all the facts.

This is summarized in the following chart:

Grade	Addition	Subtraction	Multiplication	Division
K	• invented strategies	• invented strategies		
1	• strategies	• strategies		
2	• strategies • practice leading to fluency	• strategies • practice leading to fluency		
3	• review and practice	• review and practice	• strategies • practice leading to fluency	
4	• assessment and remediation as required	• assessment and remediation as required	• review and practice	• strategies • practice leading to fluency
5	• assessment and remediation as required	• assessment and remediation as required	• review and practice	• review and practice

Table 1: *Math Facts Scope and Sequence*

Strategies for Learning the Facts

Students are encouraged to learn the math facts by first employing a variety of strategies. Concepts and skills are learned more easily and are retained longer if they are meaningful. By first concentrating on concepts and strategies, we increase retention and reduce the amount of time necessary for rote memorization. Researchers note that over time, students develop techniques that are increasingly sophisticated and efficient. Experience with the strategies provides a basis for understanding the operation involved and for gaining fluency with the facts. In this section, we describe possible strategies for learning the addition, subtraction, multiplication, and division facts. The strategies for each operation are listed roughly in order of increasing sophistication.

Strategies for Addition Facts

Common strategies include counting all, counting on, doubles, making or using 10, and reasoning from known facts.

Counting All

This is a particularly straightforward strategy. For example, to solve 7 + 8, the student gets 7 of something and 8 of something and counts how many there are altogether. The "something" could be beans or chips or marks on paper. In any case, the student counts all the objects to find the sum. This is perhaps not a very efficient method, but it is effective, especially for small numbers, and is usually well understood by the student.

Counting On

This is a natural strategy, particularly for adding 1, 2, or 3. Counters such as beans or chips may or may not be used. As an example, consider 8 + 3. The student gets 8 beans, and then 3 more, but instead of counting the first 8 again, she simply counts the 3 added beans: "9, 10, 11."

Even if counters are not used, finger gestures can help keep track of how many more have been counted on. For example, to solve 8 + 3, the student counts "9, 10, 11," holding up a finger each time a number word is said; when three fingers are up, the last word said is the answer.

Doubles

Facts such as 4 + 4 = 8 are easier to remember than facts with two different addends. Some visual imagery can help, too: two hands for 5 + 5, a carton of eggs for 6 + 6, a calendar for 7 + 7, and so on.

Making a 10

Facts with a sum of 10, such as 7 + 3 and 6 + 4, are also easier to remember than other facts. Ten frames can create visual images of making a 10. For example, 8 is shown in a ten frame like the one in Figure 1:

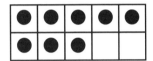

Figure 1: *A ten frame*

This visual imagery helps students remember, for example, that 8 + 2 = 10.

Using a 10

Students who are comfortable partitioning and combining small numbers can use that knowledge to find the sums of larger numbers. In particular, there are many strategies that involve using the number 10. For example, to find 9 + 7, we can decompose 7 into 1 + 6 and then 9 + 7 = 9 + 1 + 6 = 10 + 6 = 16. Similarly, 8 + 7 = 8 + 2 + 5 = 10 + 5 = 15.

Reasoning from Known Facts

If you know what 7 + 7 is, then 7 + 8 is not much harder: it's just 1 more. So, the "near doubles" can be derived from knowing the doubles.

Strategies for Subtraction Facts

Common strategies for subtraction include using counters, counting up, counting back, using 10, and reasoning from related addition and subtraction facts.

Using Counters

This method models the problem with counters like beans or chips. For example, to solve 8 − 3, the student gets 8 beans, removes 3 beans, and counts the remaining beans to find the difference. As with using the addition strategy "counting all," this relatively straightforward strategy may not be efficient but it has the great advantage that students usually understand it well.

Counting Up

The student starts at the lower number and counts on to the higher number, perhaps using fingers to keep track of how many numbers are counted. For example, to solve $8 - 5$, the student wants to know how to get from 5 to 8 and counts up 3 numbers: 6, 7, 8. So, $8 - 5 = 3$.

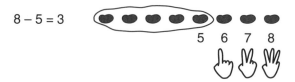

$$8 - 5 = 3$$

Figure 2: *Counting up*

Counting Back

Counting back works best for subtracting 1, 2, or 3. For larger numbers, it is probably best to count up. For example, to solve $9 - 2$, the student counts back 2 numbers: 8, 7. So, $9 - 2 = 7$.

$$9 - 2 = 7 \qquad 9 \quad 8 \quad 7$$

Figure 3: *Counting back*

Using a 10

Students follow the pattern they find when subtracting 10, e.g., $17 - 10 = 7$ and $13 - 10 = 3$, to learn close facts, e.g., $17 - 9 = 8$ and $13 - 9 = 4$. Since $17 - 9$ will be 1 more than $17 - 10$, they can reason that the answer will be 8, or $7 + 1$.

Making a 10

Knowing the addition facts that have a sum of 10, e.g., $6 + 4 = 10$, can be helpful in finding differences from 10, e.g., $10 - 6 = 4$ and $10 - 4 = 6$. Students can use ten frames to visualize these problems as in Figure 4. These facts can then also be used to find close facts, such as $11 - 4 = 7$.

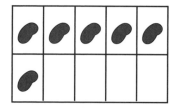

$$10 - 4 = 6$$

Figure 4: *Using a ten frame*

Using Doubles

Students can use the addition doubles, e.g., $8 + 8 = 16$ and $6 + 6 = 12$, to learn the subtraction "half-doubles" as well: $16 - 8 = 8$ and $12 - 6 = 6$. They can then use these facts to figure out close facts, such as $13 - 6 = 7$ and $15 - 8 = 7$.

Reasoning from Related Addition and Subtraction Facts

Knowing that $8 + 7 = 15$ would seem to be of some help in solving $15 - 7$. Unfortunately, however, knowing related addition facts may not be so helpful to younger or less mathematically mature students. Nevertheless, reasoning from known facts is a powerful strategy for those who can apply it and should be encouraged.

Strategies for Multiplication Facts

Common strategies for multiplication include skip counting, counting up or down from a known fact, doubling, breaking a product into the sum of known products, and using patterns.

Skip Counting

Students begin skip counting and solving problems informally that involve multiplicative situations in first grade. By the time they begin formal work with the multiplication facts in third grade, they should be fairly proficient with skip counting. This strategy is particularly useful for facts such as the 2s, 3s, 5s, and 10s, for which skip counting is easy.

Counting Up or Down from a Known Fact

This strategy involves skip counting forwards once or twice from a known fact. For example, if children know that 5×5 is 25, then they can use this to solve 6×5 (5 more) or 4×5 (5 less). Some children use this for harder facts. For 7×6, they can use the fact that $5 \times 6 = 30$ as a starting point and then count on by sixes to 42.

Doubling

Some children use doubling relationships to help them with multiplication facts involving 4, 6, and 8. For example, 4×7 is twice as much as 2×7. Since $2 \times 7 = 14$, it follows that 4×7 is 28. Since 3×8 is 24, it follows that 6×8 is 48.

Breaking a Product into the Sum of Known Products

A fact like 7×8 can be broken into the sum $5 \times 8 + 2 \times 8$ since $7 = 5 + 2$. See Figure 5. The previous two strategies are special cases of this more general strategy.

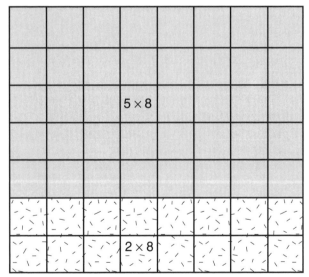

$7 \times 8 =$
$5 \times 8 + 2 \times 8 =$
$40 + 16 = 56$

Figure 5: *Breaking up 7 × 8*

Patterns

A. Perhaps the best-known examples of patterns are the nines patterns:

    1. When the nines products are listed in a column, as shown below, it is easy to see that the digits in the tens place count up by one (0, 1, 2, 3, . . .) and that the digits in the ones place count down by one (9, 8, 7, . . .).

       9
     18
     27
     36
     45
     54
     63
     72
     81

    2. The sums of the two digits in each of the nines products above are all equal to nine. For example, the sum of the digits in 36 is $3 + 6 = 9$; the sum of the digits in 72 is $7 + 2 = 9$. Adding the digits of a number to see whether they add up to nine can be a strategy in remembering a nines fact. For example, a student might think, "Let me see, does 9×6 equal 54 or 56? It must be 54 since $5 + 4$ is 9, but $5 + 6$ is not 9."

    3. The digit in the tens place in a nines fact is one less than the number being multiplied. For example, $4 \times 9 = 36$, and 3 is one less than 4. This can be combined with the previous pattern to derive nines facts. For example, 3×9 is in the twenties. Since $2 + 7$ is 9, 3×9 must be 27.

    4. Nines can easily be computed using the counting down strategy. Nine times a digit is the same as 10 times the digit, minus the digit. For example, 9×6 is $10 \times 6 - 6 = 54$.

B. Other patterns.

    Other patterns that are useful in remembering other special facts:

    1. 0 times a number equals 0.

    2. 1 times a number equals the number.

    3. 2 times a number is double the number.

    4. 5 times a number ends in 0 or 5; even numbers times 5 end in 0 and odd numbers times five end in 5.

    5. 10 times a number is the same number with a 0 on the end.

Sequencing the Study of Multiplication Facts

In kindergarten, children solve word problems involving multiplication situations. Beginning in first grade, the curriculum develops a conceptual foundation for multiplication through a variety of multiplication models, including repeated addition, the array model, and the number-line model. Fluency with the multiplication facts is expected by the end of third grade. Strategies are often introduced in specific, third-grade lessons. Practice is continued in subsequent lessons and especially in the Daily Practice and Problems and Home Practice. We do not introduce the multiplication facts in the order in which they are traditionally taught (first learning the 2s, then the

3s, then the 4s, etc.). Rather, we emphasize thinking strategies for the facts, introducing fact-groups in the following order:

2s, 3s, 5s, and 10s. The 2s, 3s, 5s, and 10s are easily solved using skip counting.

Square numbers such as $3 \times 3 = 9$, $4 \times 4 = 16$, and $5 \times 5 = 25$. These are introduced by arranging tiles into square arrays.

Nines. Students explore patterns for nines.

Last six facts. After students have learned the facts listed above and their turn-around facts ($9 \times 6 = 6 \times 9$), there are only six more facts to learn: 4×6, 4×7, 4×8, 6×7, 6×8, and 7×8.

Strategies for the Division Facts

The main strategy for learning the division facts is to think of the related multiplication fact. Therefore, students review the multiplication facts and develop fluency with the division facts by working with fact families. (Fact families are groups of related facts. An example of a fact family is $3 \times 4 = 12$, $4 \times 3 = 12$, $12 \div 3 = 4$, and $12 \div 4 = 3$.)

Using the Right Strategy

Different strategies appeal to different students. Students should not feel overburdened with the need to determine which is the "correct" strategy for a given fact. We do not intend to give them a new layer of things to learn. For example, when asked to explain a strategy for a fact, a student may say, "I've used it so much that now I just remember it." "Just remembering" is obviously an efficient strategy. The purpose of suggesting and discussing various strategies is to give students other, perhaps helpful, ways of learning the facts and to give them the confidence to think problems through when necessary. Students should have the opportunity to choose the strategies that work best for them or to invent their own.

The *Math Trailblazers* math facts program pervades most of the curriculum's components. Work with math facts are in different kinds of lessons. These are described in this section.

Math Facts Lessons

Figure 6: *Discussing fact strategies*

Everyday Work

As students work on problems in the labs and activities, encourage them to use and discuss various strategies for solving math facts problems. A number of important goals can best be reached through such discussions.

One goal is to legitimize all valid strategies, even those that may be less efficient. When students see their intuitive methods recognized and validated, they tend to perceive mathematical knowledge as continuous with everyday knowledge and common sense. We thus hope to avoid the unfortunate tendency of many students to separate their knowledge of mathematics from their knowledge of the real world.

By discussing strategies as they arise in context, students and teachers can explore how the strategies work and can verify that they are being used properly. Students should come to realize that a fact strategy that gives wrong answers is not very useful.

A second goal of our approach is to encourage students to communicate mathematical ideas. There are several reasons to stress communication: Students can learn from one another; communicating a method requires higher orders of thinking than simply applying that method; and skill at communicating is important in itself. We are social creatures. Mathematics and science are social endeavors in which communication is crucial.

A third goal of encouraging discussions of various methods is to give the teacher opportunities to learn about how students think. Knowing more about students' thinking helps the teacher ask better questions and plan more effective lessons.

Strategy Lessons

We feel that occasionally it is appropriate for lessons to focus on certain strategies that are developmentally appropriate for most students. Our plan is to begin with simple strategies that should be accessible to all students and to progress gradually to more complex forms of reasoning. For example, in the fall of first grade, we have several lessons that stress counting on to solve certain addition problems. Later, we explicitly introduce making a 10 and other, more sophisticated, strategies.

In general, you should expect your students to come up with effective strategies on their own. Our strategy lessons are intended to explore how and why various strategies work and also to codify and organize the strategies the students invent. They are not meant to dictate the only appropriate strategy for a given problem or to discourage students from using strategies they understand and like. They should be seen as opportunities to discuss strategies that may be appropriate for many students and to encourage their wider use.

Our ultimate goal is to produce students who can think mathematically, who can solve problems and deal easily with quantified information, and who enjoy mathematics and are not afraid of it. It is easier to do all of the above if one has fluency with the basic math facts. Practice strengthens students' abilities to use strategies and moves students towards fluency with the facts. Practice that follows instruction that stresses the use of strategies has been shown to improve students' fluency with the math facts. We recommend, and have incorporated into the curriculum, the following practice to gain this fluency.

Practice in Context

The primary practice of math facts will arise naturally for the students as they participate in the labs and other activities in the curriculum. These labs and activities offer many opportunities to practice addition, subtraction, multiplication, and division in a meaningful way. The lessons involve the student visually with drawings and patterns, auditorily through discussion, and tactilely through the use of many tools such as manipulatives and calculators.

Pages of problems on the basic facts are not only unnecessary, they can be counterproductive. Students may come to regard mathematics as mostly memorization and may perceive it as meaningless and unconnected to their everyday lives.

Structured Practice

Student-friendly, structured practice is built into the curriculum, especially in the DPP, Home Practice, and games. One small group of related math facts is presented to the students at a time. The practice of groups of facts is carefully distributed throughout the year. A small set of facts grouped in a meaningful way leads students to develop strategies such as adding doubles, counting back, or using a 10 for dealing with a particular situation. Furthermore, a small set of facts is a manageable amount to learn and remember.

Beginning in the second half of first grade and continuing through fifth grade, a small group of facts to be studied in a unit is introduced in the DPP. Through DPP items, students practice the facts and take a short assessment. Beginning in second grade, students use flash cards for additional practice with specific groups of facts. Facts are also practiced in many word problems in the DPP, Home Practice, and individual lessons. These problems allow students to focus on other interesting mathematical ideas as they also gain more fact practice.

Games

A variety of games are included in the curriculum, both in the lessons and in the DPP items of many units. A summary of the games used in a particular grade can be found in the Games section. Once students learn the rules of the games, they should play them periodically in class and at home for homework. Games provide an opportunity to encourage family involvement in the math program. When a game is assigned for homework, a note can be sent home with a place for the family members to sign, affirming that they played the game with their student.

Figure 7: *Playing a game*

> *Our ultimate goal is to produce students who can think mathematically, who can solve problems and deal easily with quantified information, and who enjoy mathematics and are not afraid of it. It is easier to do all of the above if one has fluency with the basic math facts.*

Use of Calculators

The relationship between knowing the math facts and the use of calculators is an interesting one. Using a multiplication table or a calculator when necessary to find a fact helps promote familiarity and reinforces the math facts. Students soon figure out that it is quicker and more efficient to know the basic facts than to have to use these tools. The use of calculators also requires excellent estimation skills so that one can easily check for errors in calculator computations. Rather than eliminating the need for fluency with the facts, successful calculator use for solving complex problems depends on fact knowledge.

When to Practice

Practicing small groups of facts often for short periods of time is more effective than practicing many facts less often for long periods of time. For example, practicing 8 to 10 subtraction facts for 5 minutes several times a week is better than practicing all the subtraction facts for half an hour once a week. Good times for practicing the facts for 5 or 10 minutes during the school day include the beginning of the day, the beginning of math class, when students have completed an assignment, when an impending activity is delayed, or when an activity ends earlier than expected. Practicing small groups of facts at home involves parents in the process and frees class time for more interesting mathematics.

> *Practicing small groups of facts often for short periods of time is more effective than practicing many facts less often for long periods of time.*

Assessment

Throughout the curriculum, teachers assess students' knowledge of the facts through observations as they work on activities, labs, and games. In Grades 3–5, students can use their *Facts I Know* charts to record their own progress in learning the facts. This type of self-assessment is very important in helping each student to become responsible for his or her own learning. Students are able to personalize their study of facts and not waste valuable time studying facts they already know.

In the second half of first grade, a sequence of facts assessments is provided in the Daily Practice and Problems. A more comprehensive facts assessment program begins in second grade. This program assesses students' progress in learning the facts, as outlined in the Expectations by Grade Level section of this tutor. As students develop strategies for a given group of facts, short quizzes accompany the practice. Students know which facts will be tested, focus practice in class and at home on those facts, then take the quiz. As they take the quiz, they use one color pencil to write answers before a given time limit, then use another color to complete the problems they need more time to answer. Students then use their *Facts I Know* charts to make a record of those facts they answered quickly, those facts they answered correctly but with less efficient strategies, and those facts they did not know at all. Using this information, students can concentrate their efforts on gaining fluency with those facts they answered correctly, but not quickly. They also know to develop strategies for those facts they could not answer at all. In this way, the number of facts studied at any one time becomes more manageable, practice becomes more meaningful, and the process less intimidating.

Tests of all the facts for any operation have a very limited role. They are used no more than two times a year to show growth over time and should not be given daily or weekly. Since we rarely, if ever, need to recall 100 facts at one time in everyday life, overemphasizing tests of all the facts reinforces the notion that math is nothing more than rote memorization and has no connection to the real world. Quizzes of small numbers of facts are as effective and not as threatening. They give students, parents, and teachers the information needed to continue learning and practicing efficiently. With an assessment approach based on strategies and the use of small groups of facts, students can see mathematics as connected to their own thinking and gain confidence in their mathematical abilities.

Conclusion

Research provides clear indications for curriculum developers and teachers about the design of effective math facts instruction. These recommendations formed the foundation of the *Math Trailblazers* math facts program. Developing strategies for learning the facts (rather than relying on rote memorization), distributing practice of small groups of facts, applying math facts in interesting problems, and using an appropriate assessment program—all are consistent with recommendations from current research. It is an instructional approach that encourages students to make sense of the mathematics they are learning. The resulting program will add efficiency and effectiveness to your students' learning of the math facts.

References

Ashlock, R.B., and C.A. Washbon. "Games: Practice Activities for the Basic Facts." In M.N. Suydam and R.E. Reys (eds.), *Developing Computational Skills: 1978 Yearbook.* National Council of Teachers of Mathematics, Reston, VA, 1978.

Beattie, L.D. "Children's Strategies for Solving Subtraction-Fact Combinations." *Arithmetic Teacher,* 27 (1), pp. 14–15, 1979.

Brownell, W.A., and C.B. Chazal. "The Effects of Premature Drill in Third-Grade Arithmetic." *Journal of Educational Research,* 29 (1), 1935.

Carpenter, T.P., and J.M. Moser. "The Acquisition of Addition and Subtraction Concepts in Grades One through Three." *Journal for Research in Mathematics Education,* 15 (3), pp. 179–202, 1984.

Cook, C.J., and J.A. Dossey. "Basic Fact Thinking Strategies for Multiplication—Revisited." *Journal for Research in Mathematics Education,* 13 (3), pp. 163–171, 1982.

Davis, E.J. "Suggestions for Teaching the Basic Facts of Arithmetic." In M.N. Suydam and R.E. Reys (eds.), *Developing Computational Skills: 1978 Yearbook.* National Council of Teachers of Mathematics, Reston, VA, 1978.

Fuson, K.C. "Teaching Addition, Subtraction, and Place-Value Concepts." In L. Wirszup and R. Streit (eds.), *Proceedings of the UCSMP International Conference on Mathematics Education: Developments in School Mathematics Education Around the World: Applications-Oriented Curricula and Technology-Supported Learning for All Students.* National Council of Teachers of Mathematics, Reston, VA, 1987.

Fuson, K.C., and G.B. Willis. "Subtracting by Counting Up: More Evidence." *Journal for Research in Mathematics Education,* 19 (5), pp. 402–420, 1988.

Fuson, K.C., J.W. Stigler, and K. Bartsch. "Grade Placement of Addition and Subtraction Topics in Japan, Mainland China, the Soviet Union, Taiwan, and the United States." *Journal for Research in Mathematics Education,* 19 (5), pp. 449–456, 1988.

Greer, B. "Multiplication and Division as Models of Situations." In D.A. Grouws (ed.), *Handbook of Research on Mathematics Teaching and Learning: A Project of the National Council of Teachers of Mathematics* (Chapter 13). Macmillan, New York, 1992.

Hiebert, James. "Relationships between Research and the NCTM Standards." *Journal for Research in Mathematics Education,* 30 January, pp. 3–19, 1999.

Isaacs, A.C., and W.M. Carroll. "Strategies for Basic Facts Instruction." *Teaching Children Mathematics,* 5 May, pp. 508–515, 1999.

Kouba, V.L., C.A. Brown, T.P. Carpenter, M.M. Lindquist, E.A. Silver, and J.O. Swafford. "Results of the Fourth NAEP Assessment of Mathematics: Number, Operations, and Word Problems." *Arithmetic Teacher,* 35 (8), pp. 14–19, 1988.

Myers, A.C., and C.A. Thornton. "The Learning-Disabled Child—Learning the Basic Facts." *Arithmetic Teacher,* 25 (3), pp. 46–50, 1977.

National Research Council. *Adding It Up: Helping Children Learn Mathematics.* National Academy Press, Washington, DC, 2001.

Principles and Standards for School Mathematics. National Council of Teachers of Mathematics, Reston, VA, 2000.

Rathmell, E.C. "Using Thinking Strategies to Teach the Basic Facts." In M.N. Suydam and R.E. Reys (eds.), *Developing Computational Skills: 1978 Yearbook.* National Council of Teachers of Mathematics, Reston, VA, 1978.

Rathmell, E.C., and P.R. Trafton. "Whole Number Computation." In J.N. Payne (ed.), *Mathematics for the Young Child.* National Council of Teachers of Mathematics, Reston, VA, 1990.

Swart, W.L. "Some Findings on Conceptual Development of Computational Skills." *Arithmetic Teacher,* 32 (5), pp. 36–38, 1985.

Thornton, C.A. "Doubles Up—Easy!" *Arithmetic Teacher,* 29 (8), p. 20, 1982.

Thornton, C.A. "Emphasizing Thinking Strategies in Basic Fact Instruction." *Journal for Research in Mathematics Education,* 9 (3), pp. 214–227, 1978.

Thornton, C.A. "Solution Strategies: Subtraction Number Facts." *Educational Studies in Mathematics,* 21 (1), pp. 241–263, 1990.

Thornton, C.A. "Strategies for the Basic Facts." In J.N. Payne (ed.), *Mathematics for the Young Child.* National Council of Teachers of Mathematics, Reston, VA, 1990.

Thornton, C.A., and P.J. Smith. "Action Research: Strategies for Learning Subtraction Facts." *Arithmetic Teacher,* 35 (8), pp. 8–12, 1988.

Van de Walle, J. *Elementary and Middle School Mathematics: Teaching Developmentally.* Addison Wesley, New York, 2001.

Math Facts Calendar
Grade 2

The Grade 2 Math Facts Calendar outlines a schedule for math facts practice, review, and assessment that roughly follows the schedule in the Unit Outlines in the *Unit Resource Guides* and in the Overview section of the *Teacher Implementation Guide.* Classrooms that are moving significantly more slowly through the units than is recommended in the Unit Outlines can use this schedule for study of the math facts to ensure that students receive the complete math facts program.

All the materials referenced in the Math Facts Calendar are located elsewhere in *Math Trailblazers* as well as the *Grade 2 Facts Resource Guide.*

The elements included in the Math Facts Calendar are described below.

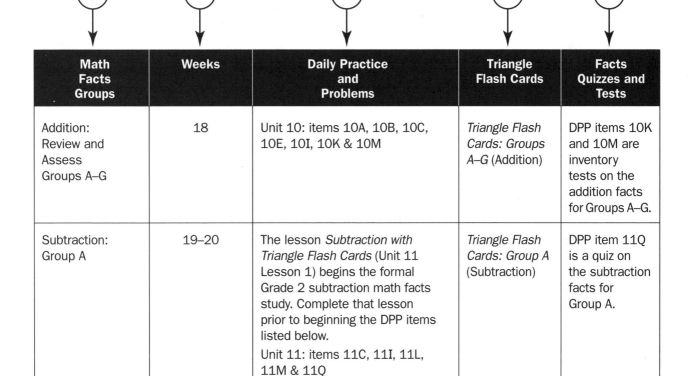

① Math Facts Groups	② Weeks	③ Daily Practice and Problems	④ Triangle Flash Cards	⑤ Facts Quizzes and Tests
Addition: Review and Assess Groups A–G	18	Unit 10: items 10A, 10B, 10C, 10E, 10I, 10K & 10M	*Triangle Flash Cards: Groups A–G* (Addition)	DPP items 10K and 10M are inventory tests on the addition facts for Groups A–G.
Subtraction: Group A	19–20	The lesson *Subtraction with Triangle Flash Cards* (Unit 11 Lesson 1) begins the formal Grade 2 subtraction math facts study. Complete that lesson prior to beginning the DPP items listed below. Unit 11: items 11C, 11I, 11L, 11M & 11Q	*Triangle Flash Cards: Group A* (Subtraction)	DPP item 11Q is a quiz on the subtraction facts for Group A.

Math Facts Groups

The *Math Trailblazers* program for practicing and assessing the addition and subtraction facts is organized into seven groups of facts. This column describes which math facts are to be reviewed, practiced, and assessed.

Weeks

Week 1 in the alternative schedule refers to the first week of school. Week 2 refers to the second week of school, and so on.

Daily Practice and Problems

The DPP items from each unit that focus on the math facts are listed in this column.

The Daily Practice and Problems (DPP) is a series of short exercises designed to:

- provide distributed practice in computation and a structure for systematic review of the basic math facts;
- develop concepts and skills such as number sense, mental math, telling time, and working with money throughout the year; and
- review topics, presenting concepts in new contexts and linking ideas from unit to unit.

The DPP may be used in class for practice and review, as assessment, or for homework. Notes for teachers provide answers as well as suggestions for using the items. Only those DPP items that focus on the math facts are listed here.

For more information on the Daily Practice and Problems, see the Daily Practice and Problems Guide in the *Teacher Implementation Guide.*

Triangle Flash Cards

As part of the DPP in Units 3–20 of second grade, students use the *Triangle Flash Cards* to practice and assess their knowledge of specific groups of addition and subtraction facts. Students categorize facts into three groups (facts I know quickly, facts I know using a strategy, facts I need to learn).

The *Triangle Flash Cards* are distributed in Units 3–9 and Units 11–17 in the *Student Guide.* Copies of the *Triangle Flash Cards* are also included in Section 6 and in the corresponding lessons of the *Unit Resource Guide.*

Facts Quizzes and Tests

Periodic quizzes of small groups of math facts are given as part of the DPP. Facts are grouped to encourage the use of strategies in learning facts. In second grade, a test on all the addition facts is given in Unit 10. A test on the addition and subtraction facts is given in Unit 20.

Grade 2 Math Facts Calendar

Math Facts Groups	Weeks	Daily Practice and Problems	Triangle Flash Cards	Facts Quizzes and Tests
Review	1–4	Unit 1: items 1A, 1C, 1E, 1G, 1H, 1I, 1K, 1L, 1N & 1O Unit 2: items 2A, 2B, 2C, 2D, 2E, 2H, 2J, 2K, 2M, 2S, 2T & 2U Unit 3: item 3A		
Addition: Group A	5–7	The lesson *Addition with Triangle Flash Cards* (Unit 3 Lesson 4) begins the formal Grade 2 addition math facts study. Complete that lesson prior to beginning the DPP items listed below. Unit 3: items 3C, 3D, 3K, 3L, 3N, 3O & 3P	*Triangle Flash Cards: Group A* (Addition)	DPP item 3P is a quiz on the addition facts for Group A.
Addition: Group B	8–9	Unit 4: items 4A, 4G, 4H, 4I, 4J & 4M	*Triangle Flash Cards: Group B* (Addition)	DPP item 4M is a quiz on the addition facts for Group B.
Addition: Group C	10	Unit 5: items 5A, 5D, 5F, 5I, 5J & 5M	*Triangle Flash Cards: Group C* (Addition)	DPP item 5M is a quiz on the addition facts for Group C.
Addition: Group D	11–12	Unit 6: items 6A, 6D, 6F, 6G, 6J, 6M & 6R	*Triangle Flash Cards: Group D* (Addition)	DPP item 6R is a quiz on the addition facts for Group D.
Addition: Group E	13–14	Unit 7: items 7A, 7C, 7E, 7G, 7I, 7K, 7M & 7P	*Triangle Flash Cards: Group E* (Addition)	DPP item 7M is a quiz on the addition facts for Group E.
Addition: Group F	15	Unit 8: items 8A, 8E, 8G, 8H, 8I & 8K	*Triangle Flash Cards: Group F* (Addition)	DPP item 8I is a quiz on the addition facts for Group F.
Addition: Group G	16–17	Unit 9: items 9A, 9D, 9E, 9H, 9I, 9K, 9N & 9P	*Triangle Flash Cards: Group G* (Addition)	DPP item 9P is a quiz on the addition facts for Group G.
Addition: Review and Assess Groups A–G	18	Unit 10: items 10A, 10B, 10C, 10E, 10I, 10K & 10M	*Triangle Flash Cards: Groups A–G* (Addition)	DPP items 10K and 10M are inventory tests on the addition facts for Groups A–G.
Subtraction: Group A	19–20	The lesson *Subtraction with Triangle Flash Cards* (Unit 11 Lesson 1) begins the formal Grade 2 subtraction math facts study. Complete that lesson prior to beginning the DPP items listed below. Unit 11: items 11C, 11I, 11L, 11M & 11Q	*Triangle Flash Cards: Group A* (Subtraction)	DPP item 11Q is a quiz on the subtraction facts for Group A.
Subtraction: Group B	21–22	Unit 12: items 12A, 12D, 12G, 12K, 12L, 12M & 12N	*Triangle Flash Cards: Group B* (Subtraction)	DPP items 12M and 12N are quizzes on the subtraction facts for Group B.
Subtraction: Group C	23	Unit 13: items 13A, 13C, 13F, 13G, 13K, 13N & 13O	*Triangle Flash Cards: Group C* (Subtraction)	DPP item 13O is a quiz on the subtraction facts for Group C.
Subtraction: Group D	24–25	Unit 14: items 14A, 14C, 14F, 14J, 14L, 14M & 14N	*Triangle Flash Cards: Group D* (Subtraction)	DPP items 14M and 14N are quizzes on the subtraction facts for Group D.

Grade 2 Math Facts Calendar *(continued)*

Math Facts Groups	Weeks	Daily Practice and Problems	Triangle Flash Cards	Facts Quizzes and Tests
Subtraction: Group E	26	Unit 15: items 15A, 15D, 15E, 15F, 15G, 15H & 15J	*Triangle Flash Cards: Group E* (Subtraction)	DPP item 15J is a quiz on the subtraction facts for Group E.
Subtraction: Group F	27–28	Unit 16: items 16A, 16B, 16C, 16E, 16G, 16I & 16K	*Triangle Flash Cards: Group F* (Subtraction)	DPP item 16K is a quiz on the subtraction facts for Group F.
Subtraction: Group G	29–30	Unit 17: items 17A, 17D, 17G, 17L & 17N	*Triangle Flash Cards: Group G* (Subtraction)	DPP item 17N is a quiz on the subtraction facts for Group G.
Addition and Subtraction: Review and Assess Groups A–D	31	Unit 18: items 18C, 18E, 18G, 18H, 18I & 18L	*Triangle Flash Cards: Groups A–D* (Addition and Subtraction)	DPP item 18L is a quiz on the addition and subtraction facts for Groups A–D.
Addition and Subtraction: Review and Assess Groups E–G	32–33	Unit 19: items 19E, 19H, 19K, 19M, 19N & 19P	*Triangle Flash Cards: Groups E–G* (Addition and Subtraction)	DPP item 19P is a quiz on the addition and subtraction facts for Groups E–G.
Addition and Subtraction: Review and Assess Groups A–G	34–35	Unit 20: items 20B, 20D, 20F & 20H	*Triangle Flash Cards: Groups A–G* (Addition and Subtraction)	DPP item 20H is an inventory test on the addition and subtraction facts for Groups A–G.

Section 5 — Facts Distribution
Review • Weeks 1–4

Math Facts Groups	Weeks	Daily Practice and Problems	Triangle Flash Cards	Facts Quizzes and Tests
Review	1–4	Unit 1: items 1A, 1C, 1E, 1G, 1H, 1I, 1K, 1L, 1N & 1O Unit 2: items 2A, 2B, 2C, 2D, 2E, 2H, 2J, 2K, 2M, 2S, 2T & 2U Unit 3: item 3A		

 **Daily Practice and Problems**

Students may solve the items individually, in groups, or as a class. The items may also be assigned for homework. The DPPs are also available on the Teacher Resource CD.

Student Questions	Teacher Notes

1A 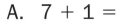 **Warm Up**

A. $7 + 1 =$

B. $5 + 2 =$

C. $3 + 4 =$

D. $3 + 3 =$

E. $2 + 6 =$

F. $3 + 6 =$

A. 8
B. 7
C. 7
D. 6
E. 8
F. 9

1C More Than, Less Than

What number is:

A. two more than three?

B. two less than eleven?

C. three more than nine?

D. three less than seven?

A. 5

B. 9

C. 12

D. 4

1E Birth Months

In a class, there are the same number of birthdays in March as in April and May combined. If there are seven birthdays in April and two in May, how many are there in March?

9 birthdays

1G  **Another Warm Up**

A. 2 + 7 =

B. 8 + 3 =

C. 4 + 2 =

D. 1 + 6 =

E. 5 + 3 =

F. 2 + 8 =

A. 9	B. 11
C. 6	D. 7
E. 8	F. 10

 1H **Number Sentence**

Write an addition number sentence with the sum of:

1. ten

2. twelve

3. seventeen

Answers will vary. Possible responses:

1. $5 + 5 = 10$; $7 + 3 = 10$

2. $6 + 6 = 12$; $10 + 2 = 12$

3. $9 + 8 = 17$; $10 + 7 = 17$

Happy Birthday

1. Five children in Helen's class have birthdays in January. Six children have birthdays in February. How many children have birthdays in the first two months of the year?

2. Nine children in Sandra's class were born in the winter. Six children were born in the summer. How many more children were born in the winter than the summer?

1. 11 children

2. 3 children

 Birthday

1. Tim and Michelle both have birthdays in October. Michelle's is five days later than Tim's. If Tim's birthday is on October 9, on what date is Michelle's birthday?

2. Gloria's birthday is fourteen days later than Dawn's. Dawn's birthday is on June 10. On what date is Gloria's birthday?

Encourage students to use a calendar to solve the problems.

1. October 14

2. June 24

Student Questions	Teacher Notes

1L More Birth Months

In Al's class, there are three more birthdays in December than in November. There are two birthdays in November. How many are there in December?

5 birthdays

1N Schools of Fish

Nancy's class counted the number of fish they had at home as pets. One student had two fish. Another had nine fish. A third had six fish. How many fish did they have in all?

17 fish

Encourage students to use counters or manipulatives to solve the problem.

1O More Animals

Jessica wants to buy a giraffe trading card and a penguin trading card. She has just enough money to buy one of each card. She has eight cents. What might be the price of the giraffe card? What might be the price of the penguin card? Find at least two solutions.

Encourage the class to find all the possible prices.

Price of Giraffe Card	Price of Penguin Card
1¢	7¢
2¢	6¢
3¢	5¢
4¢	4¢
5¢	3¢
6¢	2¢
7¢	1¢

Ask other questions like, "How much would each card be if they both cost the same amount?"

 **Daily Practice and Problems**

Students may solve the items individually, in groups, or as a class. The items may also be assigned for homework. The DPPs are also available on the Teacher Resource CD.

Student Questions	Teacher Notes

 2A Addition Facts Strategies

1. Tell whether the sum is more than, less than, or equal to 10.

   A. 5 + 5   B. 8 + 5

   C. 6 + 2   D. 4 + 6

   E. 7 + 5   F. 9 + 3

2. What is the sum of each?

1. A. equal   B. more than
   C. less than D. equal
   E. more than F. more than

Display the problems a second time and ask for the sum. Ask students to share strategies they used.

2. A. 10   B. 13
   C. 8   D. 10
   E. 12   F. 12

Strategies are discussed in the TIMS Tutor: *Math Facts* in Section 3.

 2B Ten Frame, Double Ten Frame

I will flash a number of beans on one or two ten frames. Determine how many beans there are.

Place a number of beans (1–10) on a ten frame on the overhead. Flash the light on and off. Ask students how many beans are on the ten frame. Ask them to describe what they saw. For example, if eight beans are on one ten frame, students may say they saw a row of five and a row of three. Repeat with numbers from 11–20 using two ten frames.

	Student Questions	Teacher Notes

 Which Season Were You Born In?

Larry collected data to find out in which season most of his classmates were born. His data is below.

Season	Number of Children
Winter	9
Spring	7
Summer	8
Fall	5

1. In which season were most children born?

2. How many more children were born in summer than in fall?

3. How would the data change if you included yourself in the table?

1. Winter

2. $8 - 5 = 3$ more children

3. Answers will vary.

 At the Park

1. Twelve children went to the park right after school. Six more arrived a little later. How many children are at the park?

2. Eight children are playing tag. Three children are on the swings. The rest are on the monkey bars. If fifteen children are at the park, how many are on the monkey bars?

3. Explain your strategy for either Question 1 or Question 2.

1. 18 children

2. 4 children on the monkey bars

3. A possible strategy for Question 2: counting on three from 8: 9, 10, 11. 11 at tag and swings. Then counting up from 11 to 15: 12, 13, 14, 15. 4 children on the monkey bars.

Animals Galore

1. 13 sheep

2. 14 geese

1. One flock of sheep has five lambs. The second flock has eight more than the first. How many lambs does the second flock have?

2. Eight geese were flying overhead. Six more geese took flight and joined the gaggle. How many geese are in the gaggle now?

2H **Add It Up**

Encourage students to share their solution strategies.

A. $7 + 8 =$ B. $9 + 6 =$

A. 15	B. 15
C. 14	D. 17

C. $3 + 11 =$ D. $12 + 5 =$

2J More Than or Less Than 20

1. Tell whether the sum is more than or less than 20.

   A. 12 + 6

   B. 13 + 8

   C. 13 + 5

   D. 4 + 14

2. What is the sum of each?

Write 13 + 7 = 20 on the board and use two ten frames to model this number sentence. Then, write the expressions listed to the left on the board. Ask children which expressions have a sum greater than 20 and which ones have a sum less than 20. Have students explain their thinking.

1. A. less than
   B. more than
   C. less than
   D. less than

2. A. 18
   B. 21
   C. 18
   D. 18

More, Less, or Equal

Tell whether the sum is more than, less than, or equal to 10.

A. 3 + 5

B. 8 + 2

C. 3 + 7

D. 4 + 7

E. 4 + 3

F. 9 + 5

Show one number fact at a time. Encourage children to use ten frames and apply their knowledge of sums of ten to determine whether each is more than, less than, or equal to 10. Show each problem a second time, asking for the sum. Discuss strategies used such as counting on, using a ten, and making a ten.

A. less than, 8

B. equal to, 10

C. equal to, 10

D. more than, 11

E. less than, 7

F. more than, 14

2M More Than or Less Than 20

1. Tell whether the sum is more than or less than 20. Explain your thinking.

   A. 15 + 2

   B. 16 + 2

   C. 15 + 7

   D. 6 + 16

   E. 6 + 15

   F. 3 + 16

2. What is the sum of each?

Teacher Notes

Encourage students to use two ten frames.

1. A. less than

   B. less than

   C. more than

   D. more than

   E. more than

   F. less than

2. A. 17   B. 18

   C. 22   D. 22

   E. 21   F. 19

2S The School Store

1. An eraser costs 6¢. How much do two erasers cost?

2. A sticker costs 3¢. A pencil costs 8¢. Mario has 17¢. Does he have enough money to buy a pencil and two stickers?

Teacher Notes

1. 12¢

2. yes, 8¢ + 3¢ + 3¢ = 14¢

2T My Favorite

Irma's class collected data on their favorite pizza toppings.

Pizza Topping	Number of Children
Sausage	12
Onion	7
Pepperoni	9
Spinach	1

1. Which topping is the most popular?

2. How many more children like pepperoni than spinach?

3. How many children are in Irma's class?

1. sausage
2. 8 more
3. 29 children

2U More Animals Galore

1. There is a swarm of bees in a beehive. Four bees flew out. Nine bees are still in the beehive. How many bees were in the swarm to begin with?

2. A company of parrots had some peanuts. They ate five peanuts. Now, they have two peanuts left. How many peanuts did the company of parrots have to start with?

1. 13 bees
2. 7 peanuts

Unit 3 Daily Practice and Problems

Students may solve the items individually, in groups, or as a class. The items may also be assigned for homework. The DPPs are also available on the Teacher Resource CD.

Student Questions	Teacher Notes

3A Adding Nine

A. $10 + 4 =$ _____

B. $9 + 4 =$ _____

C. $10 + 7 =$ _____

D. $9 + 7 =$ _____

E. $10 + 9 =$ _____

F. $9 + 9 =$ _____

Discuss patterns as well as strategies used. To add 9, add 10 first and then subtract 1. Using strategies like this helps students learn facts and alternative ways of computing larger numbers without repetitive drill. This strategy and others are discussed in the TIMS Tutor: *Math Facts* in Section 3.

A. 14
B. 13
C. 17
D. 16
E. 19
F. 18

Facts Distribution
Addition: Group A • Weeks 5–7

Weeks 5–7

Math Facts Groups	Weeks	Daily Practice and Problems	Triangle Flash Cards	Facts Quizzes and Tests
Addition: Group A	5–7	The lesson *Addition with Triangle Flash Cards* (Unit 3 Lesson 4) begins the formal Grade 2 addition math facts study. Complete that lesson prior to beginning the DPP items listed below. Unit 3: items 3C, 3D, 3K, 3L, 3N, 3O & 3P	*Triangle Flash Cards: Group A* (Addition)	DPP item 3P is a quiz on the addition facts for Group A.

Lesson 4

Addition with Triangle Flash Cards

Lesson Overview

Estimated Class Sessions

1

This lesson introduces a yearlong, systematic, strategies-based approach for developing fluency with the addition and subtraction facts. This lesson introduces the use of *Triangle Flash Cards* to practice the addition facts and begins work with the first group of facts.

Key Content

- Developing fluency with the addition facts.
- Practicing the addition facts using flash cards.
- Exploring the relationship between addition and subtraction.

Key Vocabulary

- sum

Math Facts

DPP items K and L provide practice with math facts.

Homework

Students take home *Triangle Flash Cards: Group A* and the *Triangle Flash Cards: Note Home* Homework Page from their *Student Guides*. They use the flash cards to practice addition facts with family members. They also take home a copy of *Information for Parents: Grade 2 Math Facts Philosophy*.

Curriculum Sequence

Before This Unit

In kindergarten and first grade, students explored the operations of addition and subtraction by using invented strategies and solving word problems. The Daily Practice and Problems, activities, and labs in Grade 1 included development of math facts strategies and ongoing practice of the facts. Daily Practice and Problems items in Units 11–20 provided systematic practice and assessment of small groups of addition facts organized around efficient strategies.

After This Unit

Daily Practice and Problem items in Units 4–10 provide systematic review and assessment of the addition facts groups. *Triangle Flash Cards* for each group are included in each unit as homework pages. Units 11–20 provide practice and assessment of the subtraction facts. See the Daily Practice and Problems Guide for this unit for the distribution of the addition facts in Grade 2. See the Daily Practice and Problems Guide for Unit 11 for the distribution of the subtraction facts in Grade 2.

Materials List

Supplies and Copies

Student	Teacher
Supplies for Each Student • scissors • 1 envelope or resealable plastic bag	**Supplies**
Copies • 1 copy of *Information for Parents: Grade 2 Math Facts Philosophy* per student (*Unit Resource Guide* Pages 11–12) • 1 copy of *Triangle Flash Cards: Group A* per student, optional (*Unit Resource Guide* Pages 59–60)	**Copies/Transparencies** • 1 transparency of *Large Triangle Flash Card* (*Unit Resource Guide* Page 58)

All blackline masters including assessment, transparency, and DPP masters are also on the Teacher Resource CD.

Student Books

Triangle Flash Cards: Group A (*Student Guide* Pages 59–60)
Triangle Flash Cards: Note Home (*Student Guide* Page 61)

Daily Practice and Problems

DPP items K–L (*Unit Resource Guide* Pages 22–23)

Note: Classrooms whose pacing differs significantly from the suggested pacing of the units should use the Math Facts Calendar in Section 4 of the *Facts Resource Guide* to ensure students receive the complete math facts program.

Assessment Tools

Observational Assessment Record (*Unit Resource Guide* Pages 13–14)

K. Story Solving (URG p. 22)

Draw a picture and write a story about 3 + 2. Write a number sentence for your story.

L. Red Buttons (URG p. 23)

Student Name	Number of Red Buttons
Elijah	8
Mikhail	4
Karl	17

A. Who has the most red buttons?

B. How many more red buttons does Elijah have than Mikhail?

C. If Elijah and Mikhail combine their buttons, will they have more than Karl?

Teaching the Activity

Display the *Large Triangle Flash Card* Transparency Master. Place three buttons on the corner with the circle. Place one button on the corner with the square. Slide the three-button pile to the third corner that is shaded. Record a 3 in the corner with the circle to indicate where the three buttons were originally placed. Repeat this process with the one button. Emphasize that the new pile shows the total number, the **sum,** of the buttons. Replace the four buttons with the number 4. Ask students to record a number sentence to show the action that took place. See Figure 9.

Next, place the buttons back in their original positions. Cover the three buttons with your hand and pose the following problem:

- *Suppose you know the total number of buttons (4) and you know that one part of the total is one button. What is the other part of the total that is hidden by my hand? What number sentence represents this story?* (4 = 1 + 3 or 4 = 3 + 1)

This particular lesson concentrates on addition sentences. However, if a student suggests a subtraction sentence to describe the action, it is a good time to reinforce the relationship between the two operations.

Repeat this process several times with other numbers, keeping the total less than six.

Use the *Large Triangle Flash Card* transparency again, this time without the buttons. Write addends in the corners with the circle and square and the sum of the numbers in the third corner. Talk with students about the idea that the same kinds of addition problems that they solved with the buttons can be solved using just the numbers. Re-create the situation by covering one of the addends and having students help write number sentences describing the action. Cover the sum and have students create number sentences representing that action. Be sure to encourage number sentences in which the sum precedes the equals sign.

Ask students to cut out the *Triangle Flash Cards: Group A* from their *Student Guides*. Ask them to compare their flash cards to the flash card on the transparency. Have students work with partners to practice the addition facts in Group A by completing the following steps:

- One partner chooses a flash card and covers the largest number (the shaded corner).
- The other partner adds the numbers in the other two corners.
- As students work through the cards, they divide the cards into three piles: those facts they

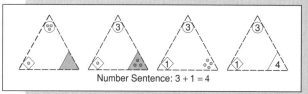

Number Sentence: 3 + 1 = 4

Figure 9: *Using the* Large Triangle Flash Card *Transparency Master*

Name _____ Date _____

Triangle Flash Cards: Group A

- Cut out the flash cards. To practice an addition fact, cover the corner with the highest number. (It is shaded.) Add the two uncovered numbers.
- Divide the cards into three piles: those facts you know and can answer quickly, those you can figure out with a strategy, and those you need to learn.
- Practice the last two piles again. Then make a list of the facts you need to practice at home.

Addition with Triangle Flash Cards   SG • Grade 2 • Unit 3 • Lesson 4   59

***Student Guide* - page 59**

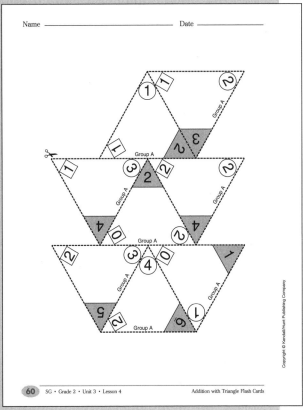

Student Guide - page 60

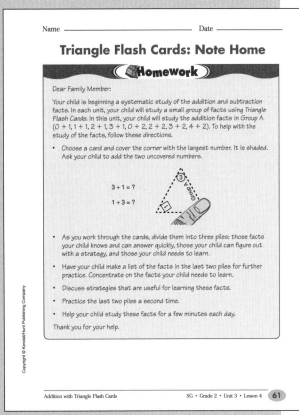

Name _____ Date _____

Triangle Flash Cards: Note Home

Homework

Dear Family Member:

Your child is beginning a systematic study of the addition and subtraction facts. In each unit, your child will study a small group of facts using *Triangle Flash Cards*. In this unit, your child will study the addition facts in Group A (0 + 1, 1 + 2, 2 + 1, 3 + 1, 0 + 2, 2 + 2, 3 + 2, 4 + 2). To help with the study of the facts, follow these directions.

• Choose a card and cover the corner with the largest number. It is shaded. Ask your child to add the two uncovered numbers.

3 + 1 = ?
1 + 3 = ?

• As you work through the cards, divide them into three piles: those facts your child knows and can answer quickly, those your child can figure out with a strategy, and those your child needs to learn.

• Have your child make a list of the facts in the last two piles for further practice. Concentrate on the facts your child needs to learn.

• Discuss strategies that are useful for learning these facts.

• Practice the last two piles a second time.

• Help your child study these facts for a few minutes each day.

Thank you for your help.

Student Guide - page 61

know and can answer quickly, those facts they can figure out with a strategy, and those they need to learn.

• Students practice again using the last two piles. Then, they make a list of the facts they need to practice.

• Partners switch roles and repeat the procedure.

• Each student stores his or her cards in an envelope, along with the list of facts that he or she needs to study, to take home to practice with a family member.

Complete the lesson by discussing strategies for solving these facts using prompts similar to the following:

• *Look at the cards with zeros. What happens when you add zero to a number?* (Zero plus any number is that number.)

• What is *32 + 0?* (32) *53 + 0?* (53)

• *What strategy did you use to add 2 + 1 and 3 + 1?* (Possible responses: Count on by one. When you add one to a number, the answer is the next number.)

• *What is 32 + 1?* (33) *53 + 1?* (54)

• *What strategy did you use to add 3 + 2? 4 + 2?* (Possible response: counting on by two.)

• *What is 32 + 2?* (34) *53 + 2?* (55)

Journal Prompt

2 + 0 = ? Explain how you know.

Math Facts

• Students discuss strategies and practice the addition facts in Group A using *Triangle Flash Cards*.

• DPP item K asks students to write a story about 3 + 2. Item L provides math facts practice.

Homework and Practice

Students study the addition facts at home using the *Triangle Flash Cards: Group A* in the *Student Guide*. The *Triangle Flash Cards: Note Home* Homework Page in the *Student Guide* provides directions for parents. Also send home a copy of *Information for Parents: Grade 2 Math Facts Philosophy* that follows the Background for this unit.

At a Glance

Math Facts and Daily Practice and Problems

DPP items K and L provide practice with math facts.

Teaching the Activity (A8)

1. Use the *Large Triangle Flash Card* Transparency Master to introduce the activity.

2. Place three buttons in one corner of the triangle and one button in another corner.

3. Move the buttons together into the third corner to show the two parts coming together to make the whole. Write 3, 1, and 4 in the appropriate corners. Have students suggest number sentences to describe the action. Write the suggested number sentences.

4. Repeat several times until students understand how the flash cards are to be used.

5. Students cut out the flash cards on the *Triangle Flash Cards: Group A* Activity Page in the *Student Guide*. They work in pairs to practice the facts in Group A.

6. Discuss strategies students use including addition of zero and counting on by one or two. Ask students to apply these strategies to larger numbers.

Homework

Students take home *Triangle Flash Cards: Group A* and the *Triangle Flash Cards: Note Home* Homework Page from their *Student Guides*. They use the flash cards to practice addition facts with family members. They also take home a copy of *Information for Parents: Grade 2 Math Facts Philosophy*.

Notes:

Large Triangle Flash Card

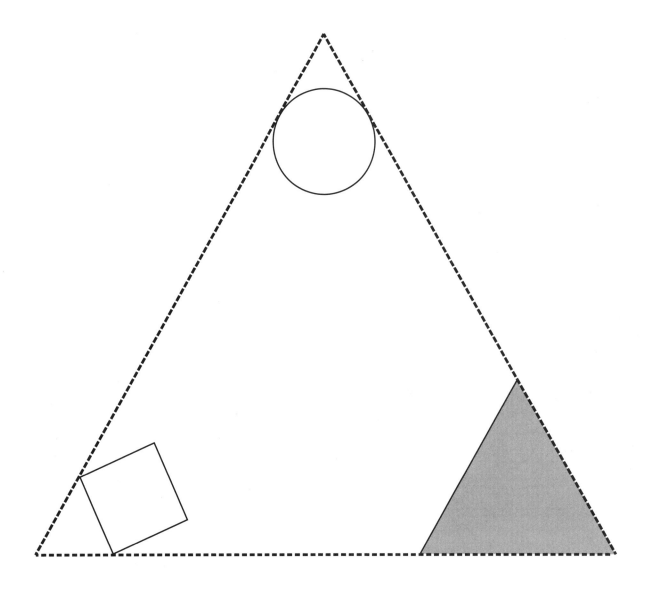

Name _____   Date _____

Triangle Flash Cards: Note Home

Homework

Dear Family Member:

Your child is beginning a systematic study of the addition and subtraction facts. In each unit, your child will study a small group of facts using *Triangle Flash Cards*. In this unit, your child will study the addition facts in Group A (0 + 1, 1 + 1, 2 + 1, 3 + 1, 0 + 2, 2 + 2, 3 + 2, 4 + 2). To help with the study of the facts, follow these directions.

• Choose a card and cover the corner with the largest number. It is shaded. Ask your child to add the two uncovered numbers.

$$3 + 1 = ?$$

$$1 + 3 = ?$$

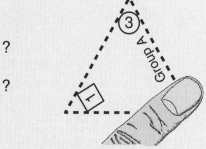

• As you work through the cards, divide them into three piles: those facts your child knows and can answer quickly, those your child can figure out with a strategy, and those your child needs to learn.

• Have your child make a list of the facts in the last two piles for further practice. Concentrate on the facts your child needs to learn.

• Discuss strategies that are useful for learning these facts.

• Practice the last two piles a second time.

• Help your child study these facts for a few minutes each day.

Thank you for your help.

Students may solve the items individually, in groups, or as a class. The items may also be assigned for homework. The DPPs are also available on the Teacher Resource CD.

Student Questions	Teacher Notes

3C Addition with Zeros

1. $0 + 1 = $ _____

2. $0 + 2 = $ _____

3. _____ $ = 3 + 0$

4. _____ $ = 4 + 0$

5. What happens when you add zero to a number?

1. 1
2. 2
3. 3
4. 4
5. Zero plus any number is that number.

3D Addition with Ones

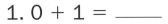

1. $0 + 1 = $ _____

2. $1 + 1 = $ _____

3. $2 + 1 = $ _____

4. $3 + 1 = $ _____

5. What happens when you add one to a number?

1. 1
2. 2
3. 3
4. 4
5. Possible response: The answer is the next counting number.

Story Solving

Draw a picture and write a story about 3 + 2. Write a number sentence for your story.

Pictures and stories will vary.

3 + 2 = 5

 Red Buttons

Student Name	Number of Red Buttons
Elijah	8
Mikhail	4
Karl	17

Encourage students to use a variety of manipulatives to solve this problem. Students might use ten frames, calculators, buttons, the *200 Chart,* and other items.

A. Karl

B. 4 buttons

C. No; 8 + 4 = 12; 17 is more than 12.

A. Who has the most red buttons?

B. How many more red buttons does Elijah have than Mikhail?

C. If Elijah and Mikhail combine their buttons, will they have more than Karl?

Student Questions	Teacher Notes

3N Addition Practice with Tens

1. $1 + 2 = $ _____

2. $10 + 20 = $ _____

3. _____ $= 4 + 2$

4. _____ $= 40 + 20$

1. 3
2. 30
3. 6
4. 60

30 Practice with Money

1. Ana had two dimes in her pocket. She found two more dimes. How many dimes does she have now?

2. How much are her dimes worth?

1. 4 dimes
2. 40¢

Addition Facts Quiz: Group A

A. _____ = 0 + 2

B. 0 + 1 = _____

C. 1 + 1 = _____

D. _____ = 1 + 3

E. 2 + 1 = _____

F. _____ = 4 + 2

G. 2 + 2 = _____

H. 3 + 2 = _____

Explain how you solved F.

A. 2

B. 1

C. 2

D. 4

E. 3

F. 6

G. 4

H. 5

Answers will vary. One possible response: counting on by two.

Weeks 8–9

Math Facts Groups	Weeks	Daily Practice and Problems	Triangle Flash Cards	Facts Quizzes and Tests
Addition: Group B	8–9	Unit 4: items 4A, 4G, 4H, 4I, 4J & 4M	*Triangle Flash Cards: Group B* (Addition)	DPP item 4M is a quiz on the addition facts for Group B.

 **Unit 4** **Daily Practice and Problems**

Students may solve the items individually, in groups, or as a class. The items may also be assigned for homework. The DPPs are also available on the Teacher Resource CD.

Student Questions	Teacher Notes

 4A *Triangle Flash Cards: Group B*

With a partner, use your *Triangle Flash Cards* to practice addition facts. Separate the cards into three piles: those facts you know and can answer quickly, those facts you can figure out with a strategy, and those you need to learn. Discuss the strategies you use with your partner.

The *Triangle Flash Cards* are located in Section 6. Ask students to work with a partner to study the facts using the flash cards. One partner covers the corner with the largest number on the card. The second partner adds the remaining two numbers.

Repeat the process with the second partner finding the sums. Encourage students to discuss the strategies they use to solve the problems. Remind students to take their cards home to study for homework. Provide an envelope for students to store their flash cards. Inform students when the quiz on the facts in Group B will be given. This quiz appears in DPP item 4M.

Addition with Zeros and Ones

1. $0 + 4 = \underline{\hphantom{00}}$ 2. $\underline{\hphantom{00}} = 0 + 5$

3. $5 + 1 = \underline{\hphantom{00}}$ 4. $\underline{\hphantom{00}} = 4 + 1$

5. $3 + 0 = \underline{\hphantom{00}}$ 6. $\underline{\hphantom{00}} = 1 + 6$

7. What happens when you add zero to a number?

8. What happens when you add one to a number?

1. 4   2. 5

3. 6   4. 5

5. 3   6. 7

7. The answer is the same as the number.

8. The answer is the next counting number.

 Story Solving

Draw a picture and write a story about $5 + 3$. Write a number sentence for your story.

Pictures and stories will vary. $5 + 3 = 8$

 Buttons

1. Joan has 3 buttons on her coat. Terry has a zipper on his coat, but no buttons. How many coat buttons do Joan and Terry have altogether?

2. Lina has 1 button on her shirt. If Aunt Betty sews 4 more buttons on Lina's shirt, how many buttons will be on her shirt?

Have students explain their strategies.

1. 3 buttons

2. 5 buttons

4J **Addition Practice with Tens**

1. 6 + 2 = ___

2. 60 + 20 = ___

3. 1 + 5 = ___

4. 10 + 50 = ___

5. ___ = 2 + 5

6. ___ = 20 + 50

1. 8   2. 80
3. 6   4. 60
5. 7   6. 70

4M **Addition Facts Quiz: Group B**

A. 0 + 3 = ___

B. 4 + 1 = ___

C. ___ = 2 + 5

D. ___ = 4 + 0

E. 6 + 2 = ___

F. ___ = 3 + 5

G. ___ = 5 + 0

H. 1 + 6 = ___

I. 5 + 1 = ___

J. Explain how you solved C.

A. 3
B. 5
C. 7
D. 4
E. 8
F. 8
G. 5
H. 7
I. 6
J. Answers will vary.
One possible response:
counting on by 2.

Math Facts Groups	Week	Daily Practice and Problems	Triangle Flash Cards	Facts Quizzes and Tests
Addition: Group C	10	Unit 5: items 5A, 5D, 5F, 5I, 5J & 5M	*Triangle Flash Cards: Group C* (Addition)	DPP item 5M is a quiz on the addition facts for Group C.

Week 10

 **Daily Practice and Problems**

Students may solve the items individually, in groups, or as a class. The items may also be assigned for homework. The DPPs are also available on the Teacher Resource CD.

Student Questions	Teacher Notes

 Triangle Flash Cards: Group C

With a partner, use your *Triangle Flash Cards* to practice addition facts. Separate the cards into three piles: those facts you know and can answer quickly, those facts you can figure out with a strategy, and those you need to learn. Discuss the strategies you use with your partner.

The *Triangle Flash Cards: Group C* are located in Section 6. Ask students to work with a partner to study the facts using the flash cards. One partner covers the corner with the largest number on the card. The second partner adds the remaining two numbers.

Repeat the process with the second partner finding the sums. Encourage students to discuss the strategies they use to solve the problems. Remind students to take their cards home to study for homework. Provide envelopes for students to store their flash cards.

Inform students when the quiz on the facts in Group C will be given. This quiz appears in DPP item 5M.

5D Math Facts 1

A. 3 + 3 = ____   B. 3 + 4 = ____

C. 4 + 4 = ____   D. 4 + 5 = ____

E. 5 + 5 = ____   F. 5 + 6 = ____

G. 5 + 7 = ____   H. 6 + 6 = ____

Make ten frames and counters available for students to use. Encourage students to describe any patterns they see that are useful in developing strategies for solving the problems.

A. 6	B. 7
C. 8	D. 9
E. 10	F. 11
G. 12	H. 12

5F Math Facts 2

A. Monjot knows 5 math facts. He wants to know 10 by next Saturday. How many more math facts must he learn?

B. Sandy learned 4 math facts yesterday. Today she is studying 4 more. How many will she know altogether?

A. 5 math facts

B. 8 math facts

5I Pennies, Nickels, and Dimes

Alice has 6 nickels. Sam has 5 nickels.

A. How many nickels do they have together?

B. How much money does Alice have?

C. How much money does Sam have?

D. How much money do they have together?

A. 11 nickels

B. 30 cents

C. 25 cents

D. 55 cents

5J Adding with Tens

A. 5 + 6 = _____   B. 50 + 60 = _____

C. 4 + 4 = _____   D. 40 + 40 = _____

E. 3 + 4 = _____   F. 30 + 40 = _____

A.	11	B.	110
C.	8	D.	80
E.	7	F.	70

5M Addition Facts Quiz: Group C

A. _____ = 3 + 4

B. 5 + 5 = _____

C. 3 + 3 = _____

D. _____ = 5 + 6

E. 4 + 4 = _____

F. _____ = 4 + 5

G. 6 + 6 = _____

H. 5 + 7 = _____

Explain how you solved F.

A. 7

B. 10

C. 6

D. 11

E. 8

F. 9

G. 12

H. 12

Answers will vary. One possible answer: doubling 4 makes 8; count on by one to get 9.

Math Facts Groups	Weeks	Daily Practice and Problems	Triangle Flash Cards	Facts Quizzes and Tests
Addition: Group D	11–12	Unit 6: items 6A, 6D, 6F, 6G, 6J, 6M & 6R	*Triangle Flash Cards: Group D* (Addition)	DPP item 6R is a quiz on the addition facts for Group D.

Daily Practice and Problems

Students may solve the items individually, in groups, or as a class. The items may also be assigned for homework. The DPPs are also available on the Teacher Resource CD.

Student Questions	Teacher Notes

 6A *Triangle Flash Cards: Group D*

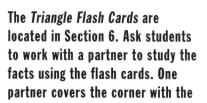

With a partner, use your *Triangle Flash Cards* to practice addition facts. Separate the cards into three piles: those facts you know and can answer quickly, those facts you can figure out with a strategy, and those you need to learn. Discuss the strategies you use with your partner.

The *Triangle Flash Cards* are located in Section 6. Ask students to work with a partner to study the facts using the flash cards. One partner covers the corner with the largest number on the card. The second partner adds the remaining two numbers.

Repeat the process with the second partner finding the sums. Encourage students to discuss the strategies they use to solve the problems. Remind students to take their cards home to study for homework. Give students envelopes to store their cards.

Inform students when the quiz on the facts in Group D will be given. This quiz appears in DPP item 6R.

6D What's the Sum?

A. $7 + 2 = $ ___

B. $6 + 4 = $ ___

C. ___ $ = 3 + 7$

D. $3 + 6 = $ ___

E. ___ $ = 3 + 8$

F. $4 + 7 = $ ___

G. $1 + 7 = $ ___

A. 9
B. 10
C. 10
D. 9
E. 11
F. 11
G. 8

After students complete the problems, ask them to describe the strategies they used. The problems that have sums of 9, 10, or 11 are grouped here to encourage the use of strategies involving the use of ten, including *using a ten, making a ten,* or *10-frame addition.* For more information on addition fact strategies, refer to the TIMS Tutor: *Math Facts* in Section 3.

6F Addition Facts Practice Using Ten

A. $8 + 2 = $ ___

B. $8 + 3 = $ ___

C. $8 + 4 = $ ___

D. ___ $ = 3 + 7$

E. ___ $ = 4 + 7$

Explain your strategy for E.

A. 10
B. 11
C. 12
D. 10
E. 11

Possible strategy: $3 + 7$ is ten, so $4 + 7$ is one more, or 11.

Student Questions	Teacher Notes

 6G   **Practice with Money** $ 7/+3

A. Vimal had 7 nickels and his brother gave him 1 more. How many nickels does he have now?

B. How much are his nickels worth?

A. 8 nickels

B. 40 cents

 6J   **Sum More**

A. ___ = 4 + 6   B. 3 + 6 = ___

C. 7 + 4 = ___   D. ___ = 7 + 3

E. 8 + 4 = ___   F. 8 + 1 = ___

Explain how you solved Question E.

A. 10   B. 9

C. 11   D. 10

E. 12   F. 9

Possible strategy: 4 = 2 + 2. So 8 + 4 is the same as 8 + 2 + 2, or 10 + 2 = 12.

6M   **Centimeters**

1. Laura's pencil is 11 centimeters long. Michelle's is 7 centimeters long. How much longer is Laura's pencil than Michelle's?

2. Find an object other than a pencil that is 7 centimeters long.

1. 4 cm

2. Answers will vary.

6R **Addition Facts Quiz: Group D**

A.   —— = 4 + 8

B.   3 + 6 = ——

C.   2 + 8 = ——

D.   —— = 2 + 7

E.   1 + 7 = ——

F.   —— = 3 + 7

G.   8 + 3 = ——

H.   4 + 6 = ——

I.   1 + 8 = ——

J.   4 + 7 = ——

Explain how you solved Question J.

A. 12

B. 9

C. 10

D. 9

E. 8

F. 10

G. 11

H. 10

I. 9

J. 11

Answers will vary. One possible response: 3 + 7 is 10 so 4 + 7 will be 1 more than 10, or 11.

Addition:
Group E

Math Facts Groups	Weeks	Daily Practice and Problems	Triangle Flash Cards	Facts Quizzes and Tests
Addition: Group E	13–14	Unit 7: items 7A, 7C, 7E, 7G, 7I, 7K, 7M & 7P	*Triangle Flash Cards: Group E* (Addition)	DPP item 7M is a quiz on the addition facts for Group E.

Unit 7 **Daily Practice and Problems**

Students may solve the items individually, in groups, or as a class. The items may also be assigned for homework. The DPPs are also available on the Teacher Resource CD.

Student Questions	Teacher Notes

7A *Triangle Flash Cards: Group E*

With a partner, use your *Triangle Flash Cards* to practice addition facts. Separate the cards into three piles: those facts you know and can answer quickly, those facts you can figure out with a strategy, and those you need to learn. Discuss the strategies you use with your partner.

The *Triangle Flash Cards* are located in Section 6. Ask students to work with a partner to study the facts using the flash cards. One partner covers the corner with the largest number on the card. The second partner adds the remaining two numbers.

Repeat the process with the second partner finding the sums. Encourage students to discuss the strategies they use to solve the problems. Remind students to take their cards home to study. Provide envelopes for students to store their flash cards.

Inform students when you will give the quiz on the facts in Group E. This quiz appears in DPP item 7M.

7C **Adding Nine**

A. $9 + 9 = $ _____

B. $8 + 6 = $ _____

C. _____ $ = 8 + 7$

D. $9 + 10 = $ _____

E. _____ $ = 8 + 5$

F. $6 + 7 = $ _____

Encourage students to share their strategies.

A. 18

B. 14

C. 15

D. 19

E. 13

F. 13

Student Questions	Teacher Notes

7E Subtracting Ten

⊞ N

A. $12 - 10 =$ _____

B. $15 - 10 =$ _____

C. $17 - 10 =$ _____

D. $11 - 10 =$ _____

E. $19 - 10 =$ _____

F. $14 - 10 =$ _____

Discuss patterns as well as strategies. Students should recognize that the answer is the digit in the ones place of the larger number. For more information on subtraction fact strategies, refer to the TIMS Tutor: *Math Facts* in Section 3.

7G Seashell Solving by the Seashore

A. Sami collected seashells at the beach in the morning. In the afternoon he collected 8 more. He had a total of 14 at the end of the day. How many did he collect in the morning? Write a number sentence and explain your strategy.

Accept either addition or subtraction number sentences. If subtraction sentences are offered first, ask for an addition sentence that also applies. Write both on the overhead or board.

A. 9 seashells in the morning; $6 + 8 = 14$. ($14 - 8 = 6$)

B. 8 stones; $7 + 8 = 15$. ($15 - 7 = 8$)

B. Toya collected 7 pretty stones on Tuesday and 15 pretty stones on Wednesday. How many more stones did she collect on Wednesday than on Tuesday? Write a number sentence and explain your strategy.

71 **Addition Practice with Tens**

A. 6 + 7 = _____

B. 60 + 70 = _____

C. 5 + 8 = _____

D. 50 + 80 = _____

E. _____ = 7 + 7

F. _____ = 70 + 70

G. _____ = 9 + 10

H. _____ = 90 + 100

I. 6 + 8 = _____

J. 60 + 80 = _____

A. 13
B. 130
C. 13
D. 130
E. 14
F. 140
G. 19
H. 190
I. 14
J. 140

7K **What's the Sum?**

A. 6 + 8 = _____

B. 7 + 6 = _____

C. _____ = 9 + 9

D. 8 + 8 = _____

E. 8 + 5 = _____

F. _____ = 7 + 7

Discuss students' strategies including reasoning from known facts. Using ten and using doubles are also efficient strategies.

A. 14
B. 13
C. 18
D. 16
E. 13
F. 14

Addition Facts Quiz: Group E

A. _____ = 9 + 10

B. 7 + 6 = _____

C. 8 + 8 = _____

D. _____ = 7 + 7

E. 8 + 7 = _____

F. _____ = 5 + 8

G. 8 + 6 = _____

H. 9 + 9 = _____

Explain how you solved Question G.

A. 19

B. 13

C. 16

D. 14

E. 15

F. 13

G. 14

H. 18

Answers will vary. One possible response: double 6 is 12, counting on 2 more gives you 14.

 **Take It Away**

A. 18 − 10 = _____

B. 9 − 3 = _____

C. 8 − 2 = _____

D. 11 − 9 = _____

E. 16 − 10 = _____

F. 13 − 10 = _____

Discuss students' strategies such as *counting up, counting back,* and *subtracting 10.*

A. 8

B. 6

C. 6

D. 2

E. 6

F. 3

Facts Distribution
Addition: Group F • Week 15

Math Facts Groups	Week	Daily Practice and Problems	Triangle Flash Cards	Facts Quizzes and Tests
Addition: Group F	15	Unit 8: items 8A, 8E, 8G, 8H, 8I & 8K	*Triangle Flash Cards: Group F* (Addition)	DPP item 8I is a quiz on the addition facts for Group F.

Daily Practice and Problems

Students may solve the items individually, in groups, or as a class. The items may also be assigned for homework. The DPPs are also available on the Teacher Resource CD.

Student Questions	Teacher Notes

 8A *Triangle Flash Cards: Group F*

With a partner, use your *Triangle Flash Cards* to practice addition facts. Separate the cards into three piles: those facts you know and can answer quickly, those facts you can figure out with a strategy, and those you need to learn. Discuss the strategies you use with your partner.

The *Triangle Flash Cards: Group F* are located in Section 6. Ask students to work with a partner to study the facts using the flash cards. One partner covers the corner with the largest number on the card. The second partner adds the remaining two numbers.

Repeat the process with the second partner finding the sums. Encourage students to discuss the strategies they use to solve the problems. Remind students to take their cards home to study for homework. Give students envelopes to store their cards.

Inform students when the quiz on the facts in Group F will be given. This quiz appears in DPP item 8I.

8E An Added Plus

A. 9 + 1 = ___

B. 10 + 2 = ___

C. ___ = 3 + 10

D. ___ = 9 + 2

E. 3 + 9 = ___

F. 9 + 4 = ___

G. 4 + 10 = ___

H. ___ = 10 + 1

A. 10

B. 12

C. 13

D. 11

E. 12

F. 13

G. 14

H. 11

8G Practice with Money

A. Tom had 4 nickels. Sam had 10 pennies. How many coins do the two boys have altogether?

B. How much are the coins worth?

C. Jack found 9 nickels in his coat pocket and 3 nickels on his desk. How many nickels did Jack find in all?

D. How much are Jack's nickels worth?

A. 14 coins

B. 30 cents

C. 12 nickels

D. 60 cents

8H **Which Is Which?**

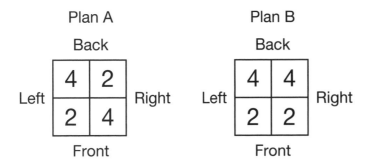

Plan A
Back

Left | 4 | 2 | Right
     | 2 | 4 |

Front

Plan B
Back

Left | 4 | 4 | Right
     | 2 | 2 |

Front

1. Which cube model belongs to Plan A?

2. Which cube model belongs to Plan B?

3. What is the volume of each cube model?

4. What is the height of each?

Build two cube models according to the plans. Display the models and the cube model plans. When you display the models, make sure that the front of each model faces the students. Students worked with cube models in Unit 6.

  3. 12 cubic units; 12 cubic units

  4. 4 units; 4 units

8I **Addition Facts Quiz: Group F**

A. $3 + 9 = $ ___

B. $1 + 10 = $ ___

C. ___ $ = 4 + 9$

D. $10 + 3 = $ ___

E. $1 + 9 = $ ___

F. ___ $ = 10 + 4$

G. ___ $ = 9 + 2$

H. $2 + 10 = $ ___

I. Explain your strategy for Question C.

A. 12

B. 11

C. 13

D. 13

E. 10

F. 14

G. 11

H. 12

I. Answers may vary. One possible strategy: add $10 + 4 = 14$, then subtract 1 (because 9 is 1 less than 10) to get 13.

8K **What's the Difference?**

A. 12 − 3 = ___

B. 14 − 10 = ___

C. ___ = 11 − 1

D. 13 − 4 = ___

E. ___ = 11 − 9

F. ___ = 12 − 2

G. 10 − 9 = ___

H. 13 − 3 = ___

Using the related addition fact is a strategy students may find helpful. Encourage students to develop and share their own strategies for the subtraction facts.

A. 9

B. 4

C. 10

D. 9

E. 2

F. 10

G. 1

H. 10

Math Facts Groups	Weeks	Daily Practice and Problems	Triangle Flash Cards	Facts Quizzes and Tests
Addition: Group G	16–17	Unit 9: items 9A, 9D, 9E, 9H, 9I, 9K, 9N & 9P	*Triangle Flash Cards: Group G* (Addition)	DPP item 9P is a quiz on the addition facts for Group G.

 **Daily Practice and Problems**

Students may solve the items individually, in groups, or as a class. The items may also be assigned for homework. The DPPs are also available on the Teacher Resource CD.

Student Questions	Teacher Notes

9A Triangle Flash Cards: Group G

With a partner, use your *Triangle Flash Cards* to practice addition facts. Separate the cards into three piles: those facts you know and can answer quickly, those facts you can figure out with a strategy, and those you need to learn. Discuss the strategies you use with your partner.

The *Triangle Flash Cards* are located in Section 6. Ask students to work with a partner to study the facts using the flash cards. One partner covers the corner with the largest number on the card. The second partner adds the remaining two numbers.

Repeat the process with the second partner finding the sums. Encourage students to discuss the strategies they use to solve the problems. Remind students to take their cards home to study for homework. Give students envelopes to store their cards.

Inform students when the quiz on the facts in Group G will be given. This quiz appears in DPP item 9P.

9D Addition Facts Practice with Ten

A. $10 + 8 =$ _____

B. $10 + 5 =$ _____

C. _____ $= 10 + 7$

D. _____ $= 10 + 6$

Discuss patterns students see.

A. 18
B. 15
C. 17
D. 16

Student Questions	Teacher Notes

 9E **Story Solving**

Draw a picture and write a story about
9 + 6.

Answers will vary.

 9H **Addition Facts: Using 10**

A. 10 + 5 = _____

B. 9 + 5 = _____

C. 10 + 6 = _____

D. 9 + 6 = _____

E. 10 + 7 = _____

F. 9 + 7 = _____

Explain your strategies for Question B.

Encourage students to share
strategies and patterns they notice.

A. 15

B. 14

C. 16

D. 15

E. 17

F. 16

Possible strategy: 10 + 5 = 15
so 9 + 5 is one less, or 14.

9I **Sharing Stickers**

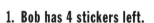

1. Bob had fifteen stickers. He used five
   on his math folder and gave six to his
   friend, Beth. How many stickers does
   Bob have left?

2. Fran bought two packages of stickers.
   Each package cost 30¢ and had
   five stickers in it. How much did Fran
   spend? How many stickers did she buy?

1. Bob has 4 stickers left.
2. Fran spent 60¢ on 10 stickers.

Student Questions	Teacher Notes

9K   **More Practice with Addition Facts**

A. $5 + 10 =$ _____

B. $10 + 8 =$ _____

C. _____ $= 5 + 9$

D. _____ $= 9 + 8$

E. $7 + 9 =$ _____

F. $6 + 9 =$ _____

A. 15

B. 18

C. 14

D. 17

E. 16

F. 15

9N **Rock and Pebbles**

James found a small rock.

1. He used a 5-gram mass and nine 1-gram masses to find the mass of the rock. What is the mass of the rock?

2. James found the mass of a second rock. He used a 10-gram mass, a 5-gram mass, and four 1-gram masses. What is the mass of the rock?

1. 14 grams

2. 19 grams

Addition Facts Quiz: Group G

A. _____ = 10 + 8

B. 10 + 5 = _____

C. 9 + 7 = _____

D. _____ = 6 + 9

E. 10 + 6 = _____

F. _____ = 9 + 8

G. 10 + 7 = _____

H. 9 + 5 = _____

Explain how you solved Question F.

A. 18

B. 15

C. 16

D. 15

E. 16

F. 17

G. 17

H. 14

Answers will vary. One possible response: 8 + 8 = 16, so 9 + 8 is one more, or 17.

Facts Distribution
Addition: Review and Assess Groups A–G •
Week 18

Math Facts Groups	Week	Daily Practice and Problems	Triangle Flash Cards	Facts Quizzes and Tests
Addition: Review and Assess Groups A–G	18	Unit 10: items 10A, 10B, 10C, 10E, 10I, 10K & 10M	*Triangle Flash Cards: Groups A–G* (Addition)	DPP items 10K and 10M are inventory tests on the addition facts for Groups A–G.

Daily Practice and Problems

Students may solve the items individually, in groups, or as a class. The items may also be assigned for homework. The DPPs are also available on the Teacher Resource CD.

Student Questions	Teacher Notes

 10A **Addition Facts 1**

A. $9 + 5 =$ ____

B. $7 + 9 =$ ____

C. $8 + 5 =$ ____

D. $5 + 2 =$ ____

E. $5 + 7 =$ ____

F. $2 + 9 =$ ____

G. $4 + 6 =$ ____

H. $7 + 7 =$ ____

I. $0 + 8 =$ ____

J. $3 + 8 =$ ____

A. 14

B. 16

C. 13

D. 7

E. 12

F. 11

G. 10

H. 14

I. 8

J. 11

Continue to have students explain their strategies for different facts. Remind them of the different strategies that help with learning the addition facts: counting up, using doubles, using a ten, making a ten, or reasoning from known facts.

Mass

Aliza measured the mass of a small pair of scissors and a plastic ruler. To balance the scissors, she used three 5-gram masses and four 1-gram masses. To balance the ruler she used one 10-gram mass, one 5-gram mass, and one 1-gram mass.

Display the appropriate gram masses to help students visualize the problem. Have students draw a picture to show their answer for Problem 2.

1. Which object has the greater mass?

1. scissors

2. Aliza placed the scissors in one pan and the ruler in the other. How could she balance the two pans?

2. Add three 1-gram masses to the pan with the ruler.

3. What masses could she use to balance two pairs of scissors?

3. Solutions will vary. Possible solution: three 10-gram masses, one 5-gram mass, and 3 one-gram masses.

10C Addition Facts 2

A. $4 + 4 =$ _____   B. _____ $= 6 + 8$

C. $8 + 9 =$ _____   D. _____ $= 5 + 6$

E. $9 + 4 =$ _____   F. _____ $= 6 + 1$

G. $3 + 7 =$ _____   H. _____ $= 9 + 6$

I. $5 + 0 =$ _____   J. _____ $= 8 + 8$

Give two related subtraction facts for
Question G.

A. 8	B. 14
C. 17	D. 11
E. 13	F. 7
G. 10	H. 15
I. 5	J. 16

$10 - 7 = 3$ and $10 - 3 = 7$

10E Addition Facts 3

A. $3 + 9 =$ _____   B. _____ $= 6 + 6$

C. _____ $= 8 + 4$ D. $6 + 7 =$ _____

E. $5 + 4 =$ _____   F. _____ $= 4 + 7$

G. _____ $= 8 + 8$ H. $3 + 5 =$ _____

I. $8 + 1 =$ _____   J. _____ $= 2 + 4$

Explain your strategy for Question C.

A. 12	B. 12
C. 12	D. 13
E. 9	F. 11
G. 16	H. 8
I. 9	J. 6

**Strategies will vary. Possible strategy: Using a ten;
$8 + 4 = 8 + 2 + 2$;
$8 + 2 = 10$ and 2 more is 12.**

10I Addition Facts 4

A. $0 + 3 =$ _____   B. _____ $= 8 + 2$

C. _____ $= 5 + 5$ D. $3 + 4 =$ _____

E. $3 + 3 =$ _____   F. _____ $= 9 + 9$

G. _____ $= 7 + 2$ H. $7 + 8 =$ _____

I. $6 + 3 =$ _____   J. $1 + 9 =$ _____

Explain your strategy for Question H.

A. 3	B. 10
C. 10	D. 7
E. 6	F. 18
G. 9	H. 15
I. 9	J. 10

Explanations may vary. One possible strategy: Doubling 7 equals 14, add one more to make 15.

Addition Facts Inventory: Groups A, B, C, and D

Solve the problems. Remember to use the different strategies you have learned to solve them.

A. 2 + 2 = _____

B. 3 + 2 = _____

C. 3 + 3 = _____

D. 6 + 6 = _____

E. _____ = 4 + 7

F. _____ = 7 + 1

G. 1 + 1 = _____

H. 6 + 3 = _____

I. 4 + 4 = _____

J. 3 + 5 = _____

K. 5 + 7 = _____

L. 0 + 3 = _____

M. 3 + 4 = _____

N. 8 + 1 = _____

O. 3 + 7 = _____

P. _____ = 1 + 5

Q. _____ = 8 + 2

R. 5 + 4 = _____

S. 4 + 0 = _____

T. 3 + 1 = _____

U. 5 + 6 = _____

V. _____ = 5 + 5

W. 4 + 6 = _____

X. 8 + 4 = _____

Y. 2 + 4 = _____

Z. 3 + 8 = _____

AA. 7 + 2 = _____

BB. 2 + 5 = _____

CC. 6 + 1 = _____

DD. 6 + 2 = _____

Answers:

A. 4　　B. 5

C. 6　　D. 12

E. 11　　F. 8

G. 2　　H. 9

I. 8　　J. 8

K. 12　　L. 3

M. 7　　N. 9

O. 10　　P. 6

Q. 10　　R. 9

S. 4　　T. 4

U. 11　　V. 10

W. 10　　X. 12

Y. 6　　Z. 11

AA. 9　　BB. 7

CC. 7　　DD. 8

10M Addition Facts Inventory: Groups E, F, and G

Solve the problems. Remember to use the different strategies you have learned to solve them.

A. 9 + 1 = _____

B. 7 + 7 = _____

C. 8 + 10 = _____

D. 8 + 6 = _____

E. 7 + 9 = _____

F. 10 + 7 = _____

G. 4 + 10 = _____

H. 2 + 9 = _____

I. 9 + 9 = _____

J. 1 + 10 = _____

K. _____ = 3 + 10

L. 8 + 9 = _____

M. 9 + 4 = _____

N. _____ = 10 + 6

O. _____ = 3 + 9

P. 10 + 2 = _____

Q. 8 + 5 = _____

R. _____ = 9 + 6

S. _____ = 8 + 8

T. 6 + 7 = _____

U. 10 + 5 = _____

V. _____ = 9 + 5

W. 7 + 8 = _____

X. _____ = 9 + 10

A.	10	B.	14
C.	18	D.	14
E.	16	F.	17
G.	14	H.	11
I.	18	J.	11
K.	13	L.	17
M.	13	N.	16
O.	12	P.	12
Q.	13	R.	15
S.	16	T.	13
U.	15	V.	14
W.	15	X.	19

Math Facts Groups	Weeks	Daily Practice and Problems	Triangle Flash Cards	Facts Quizzes and Tests
Subtraction: Group A	19–20	The lesson *Subtraction with Triangle Flash Cards* (Unit 11 Lesson 1) begins the formal Grade 2 subtraction math facts study. Complete that lesson prior to beginning the DPP items listed below. Unit 11: items 11C, 11I, 11L, 11M & 11Q	*Triangle Flash Cards: Group A* (Subtraction)	DPP item 11Q is a quiz on the subtraction facts for Group A.

Lesson 1

Subtraction with Triangle Flash Cards

Lesson Overview

Estimated Class Sessions

1

Students revisit the *Triangle Flash Cards* they used to practice the addition facts. This lesson focuses on those subtraction facts related to the addition facts in Group A.

Key Content

- Using *Triangle Flash Cards* to develop fluency with the subtraction facts.
- Using fact families to learn subtraction facts.

Key Vocabulary

- fact family
- related subtraction fact

Homework

Assign the *Triangle Flash Cards: Group A Subtraction Facts* as ongoing homework. Discuss possible strategies for learning the subtraction facts for this group including counting up, counting back, and using counters. Send home the *Triangle Flash Cards: Note Home* for parents.

Curriculum Sequence

Before This Unit

In kindergarten, first grade, and Units 1–10 of second grade, students explored the operations of addition and subtraction by using invented strategies and solving word problems. The Daily Practice and Problems, activities, and labs in Grade 1 included development of math facts strategies and ongoing practice of the facts. Daily Practice and Problems (DPP) items in Units 11–20 of first grade provided systematic practice and assessment of small groups of addition facts organized around efficient strategies.

DPP items in Units 3–10 of second grade reviewed and assessed the addition facts using the same groups.

After This Unit

Daily Practice and Problems items in Units 11–17 provide systematic review, practice, and assessment of the subtraction facts organized in the same groups. Students will use the *Triangle Flash Cards* to study the subtraction facts. All the addition and subtraction facts will be reviewed in Units 18 and 19, and an *Addition and Subtraction Math Facts Inventory* will be given in Unit 20.

Materials List

Supplies and Copies

Student	Teacher
Supplies for Each Student • envelope for storing flash cards • scissors	**Supplies**
Copies	**Copies/Transparencies** • 1 transparency of *Large Triangle Flash Card* (*Unit Resource Guide* Page 32)

All blackline masters including assessment, transparency, and DPP masters are also on the Teacher Resource CD.

Student Books

Triangle Flash Cards: Group A Subtraction Facts (*Student Guide* Pages 285–286)
Triangle Flash Cards: Note Home (*Student Guide* Page 287)

Daily Practice and Problems

DPP items A–B (*Unit Resource Guide* Pages 15–16)

Note: Classrooms whose pacing differs significantly from the suggested pacing of the units should use the Math Facts Calendar in Section 4 of the *Facts Resource Guide* to ensure students receive the complete math facts program.

Daily Practice and Problems

Suggestions for using the DPPs are on page 30.

A. Addition Practice (URG p. 15)

Solve each problem in two ways without using a calculator. Explain your strategies.

A. $\begin{array}{r} 43 \\ + 39 \\ \hline \end{array}$
B. $\begin{array}{r} 52 \\ + 48 \\ \hline \end{array}$

B. Number Sense and Estimation
(URG p. 16)

1. Roberto has 505 baseball cards in his collection. He keeps about one-half of them in a secret place. About how many cards might he have hidden: 150 cards, 250 cards, or 300 cards?

2. What number is about one-half of:
   A. 305?
   B. 181?
   C. 450?

Teaching the Activity

Use the *Large Triangle Flash Card* Transparency Master to introduce this lesson. Write 4 in the circle, 2 in the square, and 6 in the shaded corner. Ask a student to review how the cards are used to practice addition facts. Have another student record the appropriate number sentences on the board (4 + 2 = 6, 2 + 4 = 6). Repeat this a few times with other addition facts.

Next, ask the class for suggestions as to how the same card might be used to practice subtraction facts. Some students may suggest beginning with the sum and covering one of the other corners, resulting in a subtraction problem. Talk with students about how the number sentence might be recorded. For example, if there is a 4 in the circle, a 2 in the square, and a 6 in the third corner, the subtraction sentences can be 6 – 2 = 4 (covering the 4) or 6 – 4 = 2 (covering the 2). If no students suggest a way to use the cards, demonstrate this for them.

Ask students:

- *Can one card be used for more than one math fact?* (Yes)

- *How many?* (Four)

- *What are the number sentences?* (4 + 2 = 6; 2 + 4 = 6; 6 – 2 = 4; 6 – 4 = 2)

Explain to students that the subtraction facts are **related facts** to the addition facts. We call the four related facts a **fact family.**

A set of *Triangle Flash Cards: Group A Subtraction Facts* is included in the *Student Guide.* Have students work with a partner to practice the subtraction facts for Group A by completing the following steps.

- One partner chooses a flash card and covers the number in the circle. This number is the answer to a subtraction fact.

- The second partner uses the other two numbers to solve a subtraction fact and says the subtraction sentence that results.

- As the students work through the cards, the second partner divides the cards into three piles: those facts he or she knows and can answer quickly, those he or she can figure out with a strategy, and those he or she needs to learn. The second partner makes a list of the facts in the second two piles.

- The students go through the same steps again, this time covering the numbers in the squares.

- Partners switch roles and repeat the procedure.

- Each student takes home the list of facts that he or she needs to study to practice with a family member.

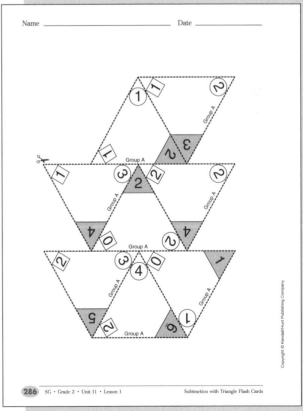

Journal Prompt

5 − 2 = ? Explain how you know.

Complete the lesson by discussing students' strategies for learning the facts. Include how knowing an addition fact helps in learning a subtraction fact.

Homework and Practice

- Assign the *Triangle Flash Cards: Group A Subtraction Facts* as ongoing homework. Send home the flash cards in an envelope along with the *Triangle Flash Cards: Note Home.* Discuss possible strategies for learning the subtraction facts for this group including counting up, counting back, and using counters.

- DPP item A provides addition practice with two-digit numbers. In item B students estimate half of a large quantity.

Name _____ Date _____

Triangle Flash Cards: Note Home

Homework

Dear Family Member:

Your child is beginning a systematic study of the subtraction facts. He or she will study a small group of facts at a time using *Triangle Flash Cards.* These are the same *Triangle Flash Cards* that your child used to practice the addition facts. They are used slightly differently when practicing the subtraction facts.

- Choose a card and cover the corner with the square. Ask your child to subtract the two uncovered numbers.

5 − 3 = ?

- As you work through the cards, divide them into three piles: those facts your child knows and can answer quickly, those your child can figure out with a strategy, and those your child needs to learn.

- Have your child make a list of the facts in the last two piles for further practice.

- Go through the cards again, this time covering the corner with the circle. Separate the cards again into three piles, and make a list of those cards in the last two piles.

- Discuss strategies that are useful for learning these facts.

- Practice the last two piles a second time.

- Help your child study these facts for a few minutes each day.

Thank you.

Subtraction with Triangle Flash Cards   SG • Grade 2 • Unit 11 • Lesson 1   **287**

Student Guide - page 287

Estimated Class Sessions

1

At a Glance

Math Facts and Daily Practice and Problems

DPP item A provides addition practice. Item B builds estimation skills.

Teaching the Activity A6

1. Use the *Large Triangle Flash Card* Transparency Master to review using the *Triangle Flash Cards* to practice addition facts.
2. Use the *Large Triangle Flash Card* Transparency Master to discuss how to use the *Triangle Flash Cards* to practice the related subtraction facts. Students solve a few problems for practice.
3. Discuss related facts and fact families.
4. Students practice the subtraction facts using *Triangle Flash Cards: Group A Subtraction Facts.*

Homework

Assign the *Triangle Flash Cards: Group A Subtraction Facts* as ongoing homework. Discuss possible strategies for learning the subtraction facts for this group including counting up, counting back, and using counters. Send home the *Triangle Flash Cards: Note Home* for parents.

Notes:

Large Triangle Flash Card

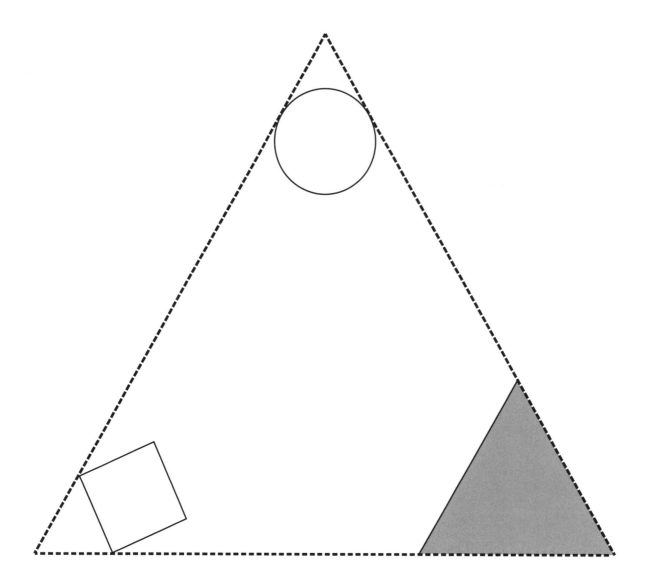

Triangle Flash Cards: Note Home

Homework

Dear Family Member:

Your child is beginning a systematic study of the subtraction facts. He or she will study a small group of facts at a time using *Triangle Flash Cards*. These are the same *Triangle Flash Cards* that your child used to practice the addition facts. They are used slightly differently when practicing the subtraction facts.

- Choose a card and cover the corner with the square. Ask your child to subtract the two uncovered numbers.

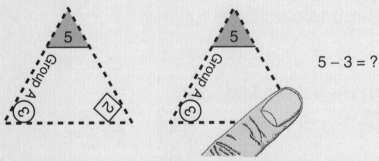

- As you work through the cards, divide them into three piles: those facts your child knows and can answer quickly, those your child can figure out with a strategy, and those your child needs to learn.

- Have your child make a list of the facts in the last two piles for further practice.

- Go through the cards again, this time covering the corner with the circle. Separate the cards again into three piles, and make a list of those cards in the last two piles.

- Discuss strategies that are useful for learning these facts.

- Practice the last two piles a second time.

- Help your child study these facts for a few minutes each day.

Thank you.

Students may solve the items individually, in groups, or as a class. The items may also be assigned for homework. The DPPs are also available on the Teacher Resource CD.

Student Questions	Teacher Notes

11C Related Facts

These four facts are related. They are called a fact family.

$$3 + 1 = 4 \qquad 1 + 3 = 4$$
$$4 - 3 = 1 \qquad 4 - 1 = 3$$

1. Write the three related facts for $2 + 4 = 6$.

2. Write the three related facts for $3 + 2 = 5$.

Encourage students to use *Triangle Flash Cards* to help them find the fact families.

1. $4 + 2 = 6$; $6 - 4 = 2$; $6 - 2 = 4$

2. $2 + 3 = 5$; $5 - 3 = 2$; $5 - 2 = 3$

11I Subtraction Practice

A. $4 - 2 = $ _____

B. $6 - 4 = $ _____

C. _____ $= 5 - 3$

D. _____ $= 4 - 1$

E. $3 - 1 = $ _____

F. $4 - 3 = $ _____

Explain your strategy for Question C.

Thinking addition may be a helpful strategy for some students. Knowing that $2 + 4 = 6$ helps in finding the answer to the related fact $6 - 4 = 2$.

A. 2

B. 2

C. 2

D. 3

E. 2

F. 1

Possible strategy: Count up 2; start at three and count up two more to 5. 4, 5.

11L Subtraction with Zero and One

A. $1 - 0 =$ _____

B. $1 - 1 =$ _____

C. $2 - 0 =$ _____

D. $2 - 1 =$ _____

E. $2 - 2 =$ _____

F. $3 - 1 =$ _____

G. $4 - 1 =$ _____

A. 1

B. 0

C. 2

D. 1

E. 0

F. 2

G. 3

Ask students to look for patterns and to explain their strategies.

11M Subtraction with Tens and Hundreds

A. $3 - 2 =$ _____

B. $30 - 20 =$ _____

C. $300 - 200 =$ _____

D. _____ $= 4 - 2$

E. _____ $= 40 - 20$

F. _____ $= 400 - 200$

A. 1

B. 10

C. 100

D. 2

E. 20

F. 200

Subtraction Facts Quiz: Group A

A. $1 - 0 =$ _____

B. $2 - 1 =$ _____

C. $6 - 2 =$ _____

D. _____ $= 5 - 3$

E. $4 - 2 =$ _____

F. _____ $= 3 - 1$

G. $1 - 1 =$ _____

H. $3 - 2 =$ _____

I. $6 - 4 =$ _____

J. $2 - 0 =$ _____

K. _____ $= 4 - 3$

L. $2 - 2 =$ _____

M. $4 - 1 =$ _____

N. $5 - 2 =$ _____

Explain how you solved Question N.

A. 1

B. 1

C. 4

D. 2

E. 2

F. 2

G. 0

H. 1

I. 2

J. 2

K. 1

L. 0

M. 3

N. 3

Answers will vary. One possible response: counting back two.

Facts Distribution
Subtraction: Group B • Weeks 21–22

Weeks 21–22

Math Facts Groups	Weeks	Daily Practice and Problems	Triangle Flash Cards	Facts Quizzes and Tests
Subtraction: Group B	21–22	Unit 12: items 12A, 12D, 12G, 12K, 12L, 12M & 12N	*Triangle Flash Cards: Group B* (Subtraction)	DPP items 12M and 12N are quizzes on the subtraction facts for Group B.

 **Daily Practice and Problems**

Students may solve the items individually, in groups, or as a class. The items may also be assigned for homework. The DPPs are also available on the Teacher Resource CD.

Student Questions	Teacher Notes

 Triangle Flash Cards: Group B Subtraction Facts

With a partner, use your *Triangle Flash Cards* to practice subtraction facts. One partner covers the corner that has a number in the circle. This number is the answer to a subtraction fact. Use the other two numbers to solve a subtraction fact. Separate the cards into three piles: those facts you know and can answer quickly, those facts you can figure out with a strategy, and those you need to learn. Make a list of the facts in the last two piles.

Put the cards back into one pile and go through them again. This time, your partner covers the number in the square. This number will now be the answer. Use the other two numbers to solve a subtraction fact. Separate the cards into three piles again. Add the facts in the last two piles to your list. Take the list home to practice.

Repeat the directions for your partner.

Discuss the strategies you use.

The *Triangle Flash Cards: Group B Subtraction Facts* are located in Section 6.

Remind students to take their cards home to study for homework. Give students envelopes to store their cards.

Inform students when you will give the quizzes on the facts in Group B. Quiz 1 appears in DPP item 12M and Quiz 2 in item 12N.

12D **Subtraction Practice**

A. $3 - 3 =$ _____

B. $4 - 4 =$ _____

C. $5 - 5 =$ _____

D. _____ $= 7 - 5$

E. $5 - 4 =$ _____

F. _____ $= 6 - 1$

G. $6 - 5 =$ _____

H. $8 - 5 =$ _____

I. _____ $= 7 - 6$

Explain your strategy for Question D.

Encourage students to look for patterns and describe their strategies.

A. 0
B. 0
C. 0
D. 2
E. 1
F. 5
G. 1
H. 3
I. 1

Possible strategy: count back 2.

12G Subtracting Zero and One

A. $3 - 0 = $ _____

B. $3 - 1 = $ _____

C. $4 - 0 = $ _____

D. $4 - 1 = $ _____

E. _____ $= 5 - 0$

F. _____ $= 5 - 1$

G. _____ $= 6 - 0$

H. _____ $= 6 - 1$

I. $7 - 0 = $ _____

J. $7 - 1 = $ _____

A. 3

B. 2

C. 4

D. 3

E. 5

F. 4

G. 6

H. 5

I. 7

J. 6

Ask students to look for patterns and describe strategies for subtracting zero and one.

12K Related Facts

These four facts are related. They are called a fact family.

$$4 + 1 = 5 \qquad 1 + 4 = 5$$
$$5 - 4 = 1 \qquad 5 - 1 = 4$$

A. Write the other three related facts for $5 + 3 = 8$.

B. Write the other three related facts for $5 + 2 = 7$.

Encourage students to use *Triangle Flash Cards* to help them find the fact families.

A. $3 + 5 = 8$; $8 - 3 = 5$; $8 - 5 = 3$

B. $2 + 5 = 7$; $7 - 2 = 5$; $7 - 5 = 2$

12L Subtraction with Tens and Hundreds

1. $8 - 2 =$ _____

2. $80 - 20 =$ _____

3. $800 - 200 =$ _____

4. _____ $= 8 - 6$

5. _____ $= 80 - 60$

6. _____ $= 800 - 600$

1. 6
2. 60
3. 600
4. 2
5. 20
6. 200

Student Questions	Teacher Notes

 Subtraction Facts Quiz 1: Group B

A. $3 - 3 =$ _____   B. $8 - 2 =$ _____

C. $5 - 0 =$ _____   D. $7 - 6 =$ _____

E. _____ $= 5 - 1$ F. $4 - 0 =$ _____

G. $6 - 1 =$ _____   H. $5 - 4 =$ _____

I. $3 - 0 =$ _____

Explain how you solved Question H.

A. 0	B. 6
C. 5	D. 1
E. 4	F. 4
G. 5	H. 1
I. 3	

Answers will vary. One possible response: counting up one.

 Subtraction Facts Quiz 2: Group B

A. $8 - 5 =$ _____   B. _____ $= 5 - 5$

C. _____ $= 7 - 2$ D. $8 - 6 =$ _____

E. $7 - 1 =$ _____   F. _____ $= 7 - 5$

G. $4 - 4 =$ _____   H. $6 - 5 =$ _____

I. $8 - 3 =$ _____

Explain how you solved Question I.

A. 3	B. 0
C. 5	D. 2
E. 6	F. 2
G. 0	H. 1
I. 5	

Answers will vary. One possible response: counting back three.

Facts Distribution
Subtraction: Group C • Week 23

Math Facts Groups	Week	Daily Practice and Problems	Triangle Flash Cards	Facts Quizzes and Tests
Subtraction: Group C	23	Unit 13: items 13A, 13C, 13F, 13G, 13K, 13N & 13O	*Triangle Flash Cards: Group C* (Subtraction)	DPP item 13O is a quiz on the subtraction facts for Group C.

Week 23

 **Daily Practice and Problems**

Students may solve the items individually, in groups, or as a class. The items may also be assigned for homework. The DPPs are also available on the Teacher Resource CD.

Student Questions	Teacher Notes

 13A *Triangle Flash Cards: Group C Subtraction Facts*

With a partner, use your *Triangle Flash Cards* to practice subtraction facts. One partner covers the corner that has a number in the circle. This number is the answer to a subtraction fact. Use the other two numbers to solve a subtraction fact. Separate the cards into three piles: those facts you know and can answer quickly, those facts you can figure out with a strategy, and those you need to learn. Make a list of the facts in the last two piles.

Put the cards back into one pile and go through them again. This time, your partner covers the number in the square. This number will now be the answer. Use the other two numbers to solve a subtraction fact. Separate the cards into three piles again. Add the facts in the last two piles to your list. Take the list home to practice.

Repeat the directions for your partner.

Discuss the strategies you use.

Triangle Flash Cards: Group C Subtraction Facts are located in Section 6.

Remind students to take their cards home to study for homework. Give students envelopes to store their cards.

Inform students when you will give the quiz on the facts in Group C. This quiz appears in DPP item 13*O*.

13C **Subtraction Facts**

A. $8 - 4 =$ B. $11 - 5 =$

C. $9 - 5 =$ D. $12 - 7 =$

E. $6 - 3 =$ F. $7 - 3 =$

G. $12 - 6 =$ H. $9 - 4 =$

Explain your strategy for Question E.

A. 4	B. 6
C. 4	D. 5
E. 3	F. 4
G. 6	H. 5

One possible strategy: 6 is double 3, so 3 is a half double:
$3 + 3 = 6$.

13F **Subtraction Story**

Write a story and draw a picture to show $12 - 5$. Write the number sentence.

Name three other number sentences that are in the same fact family.

Stories and pictures will vary.

$12 - 5 = 7$

$12 - 7 = 5$

$5 + 7 = 12$

$7 + 5 = 12$

13G Earning Money

1. Cathy earned 10 quarters shoveling snow. Her sister Anne earned 5 quarters. How many more quarters did Cathy earn than Anne?

2. How much money did Cathy earn?

3. How much money did Anne earn?

4. How much more money did Cathy earn than Anne?

1. 5 quarters
2. $2.50
3. $1.25
4. $1.25

13K Subtraction with Ten and Hundreds

1. $7 - 4 =$ _____

2. $70 - 40 =$ _____

3. $700 - 400 =$ _____

4. _____ $= 11 - 6$

5. _____ $= 110 - 60$

6. _____ $= 1100 - 600$

1. 3
2. 30
3. 300
4. 5
5. 50
6. 500

13N   **Word Problems**

A. Sol made 11 valentines and gave 6 to his friends. He gave the rest of the cards to his cousins. How many valentines did Sol give his cousins?

A. 5 cards

B. 7 hearts

Have students explain their strategies.

B. Tess had 12 candy hearts. Sandy had 5 fewer hearts than Tess. How many candy hearts did Sandy have?

13O   **Subtraction Facts Quiz: Group C**

A. 6 − 3 = ＿＿   B. 9 − 5 = ＿＿

C. 11 − 6 = ＿＿   D. ＿＿ = 7 − 3

E. 8 − 4 = ＿＿   F. ＿＿ = 12 − 7

G. 11 − 5 = ＿＿   H. 9 − 4 = ＿＿

I. 12 − 6 = ＿＿   J. 7 − 4 = ＿＿

K. ＿＿ = 10 − 5   L. 12 − 5 = ＿＿

Explain how you solved Question D.

A. 3	B. 4
C. 5	D. 4
E. 4	F. 5
G. 6	H. 5
I. 6	J. 3
K. 5	L. 7

Answers will vary. One possible response: 7 is 1 more than the double of 3; 1 more than 3 is 4.

Section 5

Facts Distribution
Subtraction: Group D • Weeks 24–25

Math Facts Groups	Weeks	Daily Practice and Problems	Triangle Flash Cards	Facts Quizzes and Tests
Subtraction: Group D	24–25	Unit 14: items 14A, 14C, 14F, 14J, 14L, 14M & 14N	*Triangle Flash Cards: Group D* (Subtraction)	DPP items 14M and 14N are quizzes on the subtraction facts for Group D.

Daily Practice and Problems

Students may solve the items individually, in groups, or as a class. The items may also be assigned for homework. The DPPs are also available on the Teacher Resource CD.

Student Questions	Teacher Notes

 14A *Triangle Flash Cards: Group D Subtraction Facts*

With a partner, use your *Triangle Flash Cards* to practice subtraction facts. One partner covers the corner that has a number in the circle. This number is the answer to a subtraction fact. Use the other two numbers to solve a subtraction fact. Separate the cards into three piles: those facts you know and can answer quickly, those you can figure out with a strategy, and those you need to learn. Make a list of the facts in the last two piles.

Put the cards back into one pile and go through them again. This time, your partner covers the number in the square. This number will now be the answer. Use the other two numbers to solve a subtraction fact. Separate the cards into three piles again. Add the facts in the last two piles to your list. Take the list home to practice.

Repeat the directions for your partner.

Discuss the strategies you use.

The *Triangle Flash Cards* for Group D are located in Section 6.

Remind students to take their cards home to study for homework. Give students envelopes to store their cards.

Inform students when you will give the quizzes on the subtraction facts for Group D. The quizzes appear in DPP items 14M and 14N.

14C Subtraction Patterns

A. 9 − 0 = _____

B. 9 − 1 = _____

C. 9 − 2 = _____

D. 9 − 3 = _____

E. 9 − 4 = _____

F. 9 − 5 = _____

G. 9 − 6 = _____

H. 9 − 7 = _____

I. 9 − 8 = _____

J. 9 − 9 = _____

Describe the patterns you see. Why does this happen?

A. 9

B. 8

C. 7

D. 6

E. 5

F. 4

G. 3

H. 2

I. 1

J. 0

The answers decrease (go down) by 1 as the numbers subtracted increase (go up) by 1.

14F Money Problems

Hank has 10 dimes and 2 nickels.

A. How many more dimes does he have than nickels?

B. What are his dimes worth?

C. What are his nickels worth?

D. How much money does Hank have in all?

A. 8 more dimes than nickels

B. $1.00

C. 10 cents

D. $1.10

14J Subtraction Practice Using Ten

Solve and write the other subtraction fact that is in the same fact family.

A. 10 − 3 = ____

B. 9 − 3 = ____

C. 11 − 3 = ____

D. 10 − 4 = ____

E. 11 − 4 = ____

F. 12 − 4 = ____

Teacher Notes

A. 7; 10 − 7 = 3

B. 6; 9 − 6 = 3

C. 8; 11 − 8 = 3

D. 6; 10 − 6 = 4

E. 7; 11 − 7 = 4

F. 8; 12 − 8 = 4

Subtraction with Tens and Hundreds

A. $8 - 7 =$ _____

B. $80 - 70 =$ _____

C. $800 - 700 =$ _____

D. $8 - 1 =$ _____

E. $80 - 10 =$ _____

F. $800 - 100 =$ _____

G. $10 - 8 =$ _____

H. $100 - 80 =$ _____

A. 1
B. 10
C. 100
D. 7
E. 70
F. 700
G. 2
H. 20

14M **Subtraction Facts Quiz 1: Group D**

A. _____ $= 11 - 4$ B. $9 - 3 =$ _____

C. $10 - 2 =$ _____   D. _____ $= 9 - 7$

E. $12 - 8 =$ _____   F. _____ $= 8 - 7$

G. $10 - 3 =$ _____   H. $9 - 6 =$ _____

I. $11 - 7 =$ _____   J. $9 - 1 =$ _____

Explain how you solved Question I.

A. 7   B. 6
C. 8   D. 2
E. 4   F. 1
G. 7   H. 3
I. 4   J. 8

Strategies will vary. One possible response is using a ten and reasoning from the addition fact $10 = 7 + 3$, so $11 = 7 + 4$, so $11 - 7 = 4$.

Subtraction Facts Quiz 2: Group D

A. 11 − 8 = _____

B. 10 − 7 = _____

C. _____ = 9 − 2

D. _____ = 11 − 3

E. 10 − 6 = _____

F. _____ = 10 − 8

G. 12 − 4 = _____

H. 9 − 8 = _____

I. 10 − 4 = _____

J. 8 − 1 = _____

Explain how you solved Question I.

A. 3

B. 3

C. 7

D. 8

E. 4

F. 2

G. 8

H. 1

I. 6

J. 7

Strategies will vary. Possible response: 6 + 4 = 10, so 10 − 4 = 6.

Math Facts Groups	Week	Daily Practice and Problems	Triangle Flash Cards	Facts Quizzes and Tests
Subtraction: Group E	26	Unit 15: items 15A, 15D, 15E, 15F, 15G, 15H & 15J	*Triangle Flash Cards: Group E* (Subtraction)	DPP item 15J is a quiz on the subtraction facts for Group E.

Unit 15 Daily Practice and Problems

Students may solve the items individually, in groups, or as a class. The items may also be assigned for homework. The DPPs are also available on the Teacher Resource CD.

Student Questions	Teacher Notes

15A *Triangle Flash Cards: Group E Subtraction Facts*

With a partner, use your *Triangle Flash Cards* to practice subtraction facts. One partner covers the corner that has a number in the circle. This number is the answer to a subtraction fact. Use the other two numbers to solve a subtraction fact. Separate the cards into three piles: those facts you know and can answer quickly, those you can figure out with a strategy, and those you need to learn. Make a list of the facts in the last two piles.

Put the cards back into one pile and go through them again. This time, your partner covers the number in the square. This number will now be the answer. Use the other two numbers to solve a subtraction fact. Separate the cards into three piles again. Add the facts in the last two piles to your list. Take the list home to practice.

Repeat the directions for your partner.

Discuss the strategies you use.

The *Triangle Flash Cards: Group E* are located in Section 6.

Remind students to take their cards home to study for homework. Give students envelopes to store their cards.

Inform students when you will give the quiz on the facts in Group E. This quiz appears in DPP item 15J.

Student Questions	**Teacher Notes**

15D Related Facts

These four facts are related. They are called a fact family.

$6 + 8 = 14$, $8 + 6 = 14$, $14 - 8 = 6$, $14 - 6 = 8$

1. Write the three related facts for $7 + 8 = 15$.

2. Write the three related facts for $6 + 7 = 13$.

Encourage students to use *Triangle Flash Cards* to help them find the fact families.

1. $8 + 7 = 15$, $15 - 8 = 7$, $15 - 7 = 8$

2. $7 + 6 = 13$, $13 - 7 = 6$, $13 - 6 = 7$

15E Addition

A. $60 + 70 =$ B. $70 + 70 =$

C. $80 + 70 =$ D. $80 + 80 =$

E. $60 + 80 =$ F. $90 + 90 =$

A. 130   B. 140

C. 150   D. 160

E. 140   F. 180

15F Subtraction Practice

A. $14 - 7 =$ _____

B. $15 - 7 =$ _____

C. _____ $= 13 - 7$

D. _____ $= 16 - 8$

E. $15 - 8 =$ _____

F. $14 - 8 =$ _____

Explain your strategy for Question C.

A. 7

B. 8

C. 6

D. 8

E. 7

F. 6

A possible strategy is using doubles: $14 - 7 = 7$, so $13 - 7$ is one less, 6. Encourage students to share their own strategies.

Student Questions	Teacher Notes

15G **More Subtraction Practice**

A. $18 - 9 =$ _____

B. _____ $= 19 - 10$

C. _____ $= 19 - 9$

D. $13 - 5 =$ _____

E. _____ $= 13 - 6$

F. $14 - 6 =$ _____

G. $13 - 8 =$ _____

Explain your strategy for Question F.

A. 9

B. 9

C. 10

D. 8

E. 7

F. 8

G. 5

A possible strategy is using doubles: $12 - 6 = 6$, so $14 - 6$ is two more, 8. Encourage students to share their own strategies.

 15H **Story Solving**

Draw a picture and make up a story for $13 - 8$.

Stories will vary.

15J Subtraction Facts Quiz: Group E

A. 19 − 10 = _____

B. 13 − 6 = _____

C. _____ = 14 − 8

D. _____ = 15 − 7

E. 19 − 9 = _____

F. 14 − 7 = _____

G. _____ = 13 − 5

H. 16 − 8 = _____

I. 18 − 9 = _____

J. 13 − 7 = _____

K. _____ = 15 − 8

L. 13 − 8 = _____

M. 14 − 6 = _____

Explain how you solved Question D.

A. 9
B. 7
C. 6
D. 8
E. 10
F. 7
G. 8
H. 8
I. 9
J. 6
K. 7
L. 5
M. 8

Strategies will vary. Possible response: 14 − 7 is 7, so 15 − 7 is one more, 8.

Facts Distribution
Subtraction: Group F • Weeks 27–28

Math Facts Groups	Weeks	Daily Practice and Problems	Triangle Flash Cards	Facts Quizzes and Tests
Subtraction: Group F	27–28	Unit 16: items 16A, 16B, 16C, 16E, 16G, 16I & 16K	*Triangle Flash Cards: Group F* (Subtraction)	DPP item 16K is a quiz on the subtraction facts for Group F.

 **Daily Practice and Problems**

Students may solve the items individually, in groups, or as a class. The items may also be assigned for homework. The DPPs are also available on the Teacher Resource CD.

Student Questions	Teacher Notes

 Triangle Flash Cards: Group F Subtraction Facts

With a partner, use your *Triangle Flash Cards* to practice subtraction facts. One partner covers the corner that has a number in the circle. This number is the answer to a subtraction fact. Use the other two numbers to solve a subtraction fact. Separate the cards into three piles: those facts you know and can answer quickly, those you can figure out with a strategy, and those you need to learn. Make a list of the facts in the last two piles.

Put the cards back into one pile and go through them again. This time, your partner covers the number in the square. This number will now be the answer. Use the other two numbers to solve a subtraction fact. Separate the cards into three piles again. Add the facts in the last two piles to your list. Take the list home to practice.

Repeat the directions for your partner.

Discuss the strategies you use.

The *Triangle Flash Cards* are located in Section 6.

Remind students to take their cards home to study for homework. Give students envelopes to store their cards.

Inform students when you will give the quiz on the facts in Group F. This quiz appears in DPP item 16K.

16B Addition Facts

A. $9 + 1 =$ B. $90 + 10 =$

C. $9 + 2 =$ D. $90 + 20 =$

E. $9 + 3 =$ F. $90 + 30 =$

A. 10   B. 100
C. 11   D. 110
E. 12   F. 120

16C Subtraction Facts and Families

Write the answers. Draw a line between facts that are part of the same fact family.

A. $11 - 2 =$ B. $13 - 3 =$

C. $12 - 9 =$ D. $11 - 9 =$

E. $10 - 1 =$ F. $10 - 9 =$

G. $13 - 10 =$ H. $12 - 3 =$

Discuss students' strategies.

A. 9   B. 10
C. 3   D. 2
E. 9   F. 1
G. 3   H. 9

16E **More Subtraction Facts and Families**

Write the answers. Draw a line between facts that are part of the same fact family.

A. $14 - 10 =$

B. $11 - 10 =$

C. $11 - 1 =$

D. $13 - 4 =$

E. $12 - 2 =$

F. $14 - 4 =$

G. $13 - 9 =$

H. $12 - 10 =$

Discuss students' strategies.

A. 4   B. 1
C. 10   D. 9
E. 10   F. 10
G. 4   H. 2

16G **Money to Spend**

1. Frank had 120 pennies to spend. He bought a valentine card for 90 cents. How much money did he have left? Write a number sentence.

2. Ernest had 140 pennies to spend. He bought a pack of gum for 40 cents. How much money did he have left? Write a number sentence.

1. 30 cents; $120 - 90 =$ 30 cents

2. 100 cents or $1.00; $140 - 40 = 100$ cents

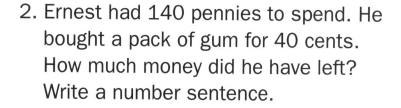

161 **Subtraction with Tens and Hundreds**

A. $13 - 4 =$

B. $130 - 40 =$

C. $1300 - 400 =$

D. $11 - 9 =$

E. $110 - 90 =$

F. $1100 - 900 =$

A. 9
B. 90
C. 900
D. 2
E. 20
F. 200

16K *Subtraction Facts Quiz: Group F*

A. 13 − 3 =   B. 11 − 9 =

C. 10 − 1 =   D. 12 − 10 =

E. 13 − 10 =   F. 11 − 10 =

G. 13 − 9 =   H. 14 − 4 =

I. 10 − 9 =   J. 11 − 2 =

K. 12 − 9 =   L. 13 − 4 =

M. 14 − 10 =   N. 12 − 3 =

O. 11 − 1 =   P. 12 − 2 =

Explain your strategy for Question G.

A. 10   B. 2
C. 9   D. 2
E. 3   F. 1
G. 4   H. 10
I. 1   J. 9
K. 3   L. 9
M. 4   N. 9
O. 10   P. 10

Strategies will vary. One possible strategy is: 13 − 10 = 3, so 13 − 9 is 4.

Math Facts Groups	Weeks	Daily Practice and Problems	Triangle Flash Cards	Facts Quizzes and Tests
Subtraction: Group G	29–30	Unit 17: items 17A, 17D, 17G, 17L & 17N	*Triangle Flash Cards: Group G* (Subtraction)	DPP item 17N is a quiz on the subtraction facts for Group G.

 **Unit 17** **Daily Practice and Problems**

Students may solve the items individually, in groups, or as a class. The items may also be assigned for homework. The DPPs are also available on the Teacher Resource CD.

Student Questions	Teacher Notes

 Triangle Flash Cards: Group G Subtraction Facts

With a partner, use your *Triangle Flash Cards* to practice subtraction facts. One partner covers the corner that has a number in the circle. This number is the answer to a subtraction fact. Use the other two numbers to solve a subtraction fact. Separate the cards into three piles: those facts you know and can answer quickly, those you can figure out with a strategy, and those you need to learn. Make a list of the facts in the last two piles.

Put the cards back into one pile and go through them again. This time, your partner covers the number in the square. This number will now be the answer. Use the other two numbers to solve a subtraction fact. Separate the cards into three piles again. Add the facts in the last two piles to your list. Take the list home to practice.

Repeat the directions for your partner.

Discuss the strategies you use.

The *Triangle Flash Cards* are located in Section 6.

Remind students to take their cards home to study for homework. Give students envelopes to store their cards.

Inform students when you will give the quiz on the subtraction facts for Group G. This quiz appears in DPP item 17N.

Subtraction Facts Practice

A. $17 - 10 =$ _____

B. $17 - 9 =$ _____

C. _____ $= 15 - 10$

D. _____ $= 15 - 9$

E. $16 - 10 =$ _____

F. $16 - 9 =$ _____

G. $14 - 9 =$ _____

H. $18 - 8 =$ _____

Explain your strategy for Question G.

A. 7

B. 8

C. 5

D. 6

E. 6

F. 7

G. 5

H. 10

Possible strategy: Think of ten.
$14 - 10 = 4$, so $14 - 9$ is one
more, 5.

 Word Problem

1. Jenny collected 9 stickers. Tim gave her 7 more for her collection. How many stickers are in Jenny's collection now?

2. Jenny made a birthday card for her mother using 6 stickers from her collection. How many stickers are in Jenny's collection now?

1. 16 stickers, $9 + 7 = 16$
2. 10 stickers, $16 - 6 = 10$

More Subtraction Facts Practice

A. $18 - 10 =$ _____

B. _____ $= 14 - 5$

C. _____ $= 17 - 8$

D. $15 - 5 =$ _____

E. $17 - 7 =$ _____

F. $16 - 6 =$ _____

G. _____ $= 15 - 6$

H. _____ $= 16 - 7$

Write the related addition and subtraction facts for Questions G and H.

A. 8   B. 9

C. 9   D. 10

E. 10   F. 10

G. 9   H. 9

$15 - 6 = 9$: $15 - 9 = 6$,
$9 + 6 = 15$, $6 + 9 = 15$

$16 - 7 = 9$: $16 - 9 = 7$,
$7 + 9 = 16$, $9 + 7 = 16$

17N Subtraction Facts Quiz: Group G

A. $18 - 8 =$ _____

B. $16 - 7 =$ _____

C. $15 - 10 =$ _____

D. _____ $= 17 - 7$

E. _____ $= 15 - 9$

F. $14 - 9 =$ _____

G. $17 - 9 =$ _____

H. _____ $= 14 - 5$

I. $15 - 6 =$ _____

J. $18 - 10 =$ _____

K. $16 - 9 =$ _____

L. $15 - 5 =$ _____

M. _____ $= 17 - 10$

N. _____ $= 16 - 10$

O. $16 - 6 =$ _____

P. $17 - 8 =$ _____

Explain how you solved Question E.

Teacher Notes

A. 10
B. 9
C. 5
D. 10
E. 6
F. 5
G. 8
H. 9
I. 9
J. 8
K. 7
L. 10
M. 7
N. 6
O. 10
P. 9

Answers will vary. One possible strategy: Use a ten. $15 - 10 = 5$, so $15 - 9$ is taking away one less, 6.

Facts Distribution

Addition and Subtraction: Review and Assess
Groups A–D • Week 31

Math Facts Groups	Week	Daily Practice and Problems	Triangle Flash Cards	Facts Quizzes and Tests
Addition and Subtraction: Review and Assess Groups A–D	31	Unit 18: items 18C, 18E, 18G, 18H, 18I & 18L	*Triangle Flash Cards: Groups A–D* (Addition and Subtraction)	DPP item 18L is a quiz on the addition and subtraction facts for Groups A–D.

Unit 18 · Daily Practice and Problems

Students may solve the items individually, in groups, or as a class. The items may also be assigned for homework. The DPPs are also available on the Teacher Resource CD.

Student Questions	Teacher Notes

18C   Addition and Subtraction Facts 1

Solve these problems in your head.

A. 20 + 20 =

B. 40 + 40 =

C. 50 + 40 =

D. 60 + 30 =

E. 50 − 20 =

F. 60 − 40 =

G. 60 + 50 =

H. 80 − 30 =

A. 40   B. 80

C. 90   D. 90

E. 30   F. 20

G. 110   H. 50

18E   Subtraction Facts Problems

Solve the problems and write a number sentence for each.

A. Jane counted 11 days until her cousin was coming to play. Three days passed. Now, how many days until Jane's cousin comes?

B. Jean is 3 years old. Her brother Jon is 7 years old. How many years older is Jon than Jean?

C. June has 3 eggs. She needs 6 eggs to make a double batch of cookies. How many more eggs does June need?

These questions show three different subtraction concepts. Effective strategies include counting up, counting back, and using doubles. Students may write either addition or subtraction number sentences.

A. 8 days; 11 − 3 = 8 days or 3 + 8 = 11 days

B. 4 years; 7 − 3 = 4 years or 3 + 4 = 7 years

C. 3 eggs; 6 − 3 = 3 eggs or 3 + 3 = 6 eggs

18G   Addition and Subtraction Facts 2

A. $2 + 8 =$ _____   B. $7 = 5 +$ _____

C. $12 - 7 =$ _____   D. _____ $= 5 + 5$

E. $2 = 2 -$ _____   F. $7 + 3 =$ _____

G. _____ $= 4 + 8$ H. $8 - 6 =$ _____

I. $11 - 7 =$ _____   J. $5 = 4 +$ _____

Explain your strategy for Question I.

A. 10   B. 2

C. 5   D. 10

E. 0   F. 10

G. 12   H. 2

I. 4   J. 1

Answers will vary. Possible strategy: Since $10 - 7 = 3$, $11 - 7$ is one more or 4.

18H   Fractions

1. Wayne made a shape with square-inch tiles. Half of his shape was made from 6 tiles. How many tiles did Wayne use to create his shape?

2. Darcy made a shape, too. One-third of the tiles in her shape were yellow. She used 2 yellow tiles. How many tiles did Darcy use to create her shape?

Remind students of their work with fractions and square-inch tiles in Unit 14. Display square-inch tiles on the overhead. Ask volunteers to solve the problems using tiles.

1. 12 tiles

2. 6 tiles

18I Addition and Subtraction Facts 3

A. $5 + 0 =$ _____   B. $10 = 6 +$ _____

C. $4 - 3 =$ _____   D. _____ $= 7 - 1$

E. $7 = 9 -$ _____   F. $7 + 1 =$ _____

G. _____ $= 4 + 0$ H. $11 - 6 =$ _____

I. $11 - 8 =$ _____   J. $6 - 1 =$ _____

Explain your strategy for Question H.

A. 5   B. 4
C. 1   D. 6
E. 2   F. 8
G. 4   H. 5
I. 3   J. 5

Answers will vary. Possible strategy:
$12 - 6 = 6$, so $11 - 6$ is one less
or 5.

18L Addition and Subtraction Facts Quiz

A. $5 + 7 =$ _____   B. $12 - 4 =$ _____

C. $7 + 4 =$ _____   D. _____ $= 2 + 6$

E. $10 - 5 =$ _____   F. $5 + 6 =$ _____

G. _____ $= 4 - 4$ H. $4 + 4 =$ _____

I. $9 - 5 =$ _____   J. _____ $= 5 + 3$

K. _____ $= 9 - 7$ L. $8 - 1 =$ _____

M. $9 - 3 =$ _____   N. _____ $= 10 - 2$

O. $4 - 2 =$ _____   P. $0 + 5 =$ _____

Q. _____ $= 4 + 6$ R. $11 - 3 =$ _____

S. $10 - 7 =$ _____   T. $12 - 6 =$ _____

U. $7 - 1 =$ _____   V. _____ $= 7 - 3$

W. $3 +$ _____ $= 6$ X. $5 - 2 =$ _____

Y. _____ $= 7 - 5$ Z. $6 - 5 =$ _____

Explain your strategy for Question P.

A. 12   B. 8
C. 11   D. 8
E. 5   F. 11
G. 0   H. 8
I. 4   J. 8
K. 2   L. 7
M. 6   N. 8
O. 2   P. 5
Q. 10   R. 8
S. 3   T. 6
U. 6   V. 4
W. 3   X. 3
Y. 2   Z. 1

**Possible response: Any number plus
zero is just that number.**

Math Facts Groups	Weeks	Daily Practice and Problems	Triangle Flash Cards	Facts Quizzes and Tests
Addition and Subtraction: Review and Assess Groups E–G	32–33	Unit 19: items 19E, 19H, 19K, 19M, 19N & 19P	*Triangle Flash Cards: Groups E–G* (Addition and Subtraction)	DPP item 19P is a quiz on the addition and subtraction facts for Groups E–G.

Unit 19 Daily Practice and Problems

Students may solve the items individually, in groups, or as a class. The items may also be assigned for homework. The DPPs are also available on the Teacher Resource CD.

Student Questions	Teacher Notes

19E Subtraction Practice 1

1. $16 - 7 =$ _____

2. $10 - 9 =$ _____

3. $14 - 5 =$ _____

4. $7 +$ _____ $= 15$

5. $14 - 4 =$ _____

6. $15 - 6 =$ _____

7. _____ $= 12 - 9$

8. _____ $+ 8 = 18$

9. _____ $= 6 + 7$

10. $14 - 8 =$ _____

Explain the strategy you used for Question 4.

Teacher Notes:

1. 9   2. 1
3. 9   4. 8
5. 10   6. 9
7. 3   8. 10
9. 13   10. 6

Answers will vary. Possible strategy: Double 7, $7 + 7 = 14$, so $7 + 8$ is 15.

19H Subtraction Practice 2

A. $8 + 8 =$ _____

B. $13 - 3 =$ _____

C. $11 - 10 =$ _____

D. _____ $= 7 + 10$

E. $6 + 10 =$ _____

F. $11 -$ _____ $= 9$

G. $12 - 2 =$ _____

H. $18 - 9 =$ _____

I. $10 + 5 =$ _____

J. Write the three facts related to $8 + 9$.

Teacher Notes:

A. 16
B. 10
C. 1
D. 17
E. 16
F. 2
G. 10
H. 9
I. 15
J. $9 + 8 = 17$
   $17 - 9 = 8$
   $17 - 8 = 9$

Making Shapes

9 sq cm

Roberto drew a shape with an area of 19 square centimeters on *Centimeter Grid Paper.* His shape was 10 square centimeters larger than Jerome's shape. What was the area of Jerome's shape?

 Addition Story

Pictures and stories will vary.

$8 + 7 = 15$

Draw a picture and write a story about $8 + 7$. Include a number sentence in your story.

 Word Problems at the Beach

Write a number sentence for each problem.

1. 9 shells; $13 - 4 = 9$ shells or $4 + 9 = 13$ shells

2. 8 shells; $13 - 5 = 8$ shells or $5 + 8 = 13$ shells

3. At least 7 shells; $7 + 7 = 14$ or $14 - 7 = 7$

1. Heather collected 13 shells in her bucket at the beach. During her walk 4 shells broke. How many whole shells does Heather have?

2. Linda collected 13 shells and her brother Jimmy collected 5. How many more shells did Linda collect than Jimmy?

3. Howard collected 7 shells. He wanted to collect more shells than Linda. How many more shells does he need to collect?

19P **Addition and Subtraction Facts Quiz**

A. 14 − 7 = ___   B. 7 + 8 = ___

C. 5 + ___ = 13   D. 11 = ___ + 2

E. ___ = 9 + 9   F. 13 − 10 = ___

G. 17 − 7 = ___   H. 6 + ___ = 13

I. 2 + 10 = ___   J. 6 + 8 = ___

K. 8 + ___ = 16   L. 10 − 1 = ___

M. ___ + 10 = 16   N. 9 + 5 = ___

O. ___ = 14 − 10   P. 17 = ___ + 9

Q. 19 − 9 = ___   R. 3 + 9 = ___

S. 10 + ___ = 15   T. 13 − 4 = ___

U. 10 + 1 = ___   V. 15 − 9 = ___

W. 7 + 9 = ___   X. ___ = 18 − 10

Explain your strategy for Question P.

A. 7	B. 15
C. 8	D. 9
E. 18	F. 3
G. 10	H. 7
I. 12	J. 14
K. 8	L. 9
M. 6	N. 14
O. 4	P. 8
Q. 10	R. 12
S. 5	T. 9
U. 11	V. 6
W. 16	X. 8

Answers will vary. One possible response: 9 + 9 = 18, so 9 + 8 is one less, 17.

Facts Distribution

Addition and Subtraction: Review and Assess
Groups A–G • Weeks 34–35

Math Facts Groups	Weeks	Daily Practice and Problems	Triangle Flash Cards	Facts Quizzes and Tests
Addition and Subtraction: Review and Assess Groups A–G	34–35	Unit 20: items 20B, 20D, 20F & 20H	*Triangle Flash Cards: Groups A–G* (Addition and Subtraction)	DPP item 20H is an inventory test on the addition and subtraction facts for Groups A–G.

Unit 20 Daily Practice and Problems

Students may solve the items individually, in groups, or as a class. The items may also be assigned for homework. The DPPs are also available on the Teacher Resource CD.

Student Questions	Teacher Notes
20B Addition and Subtraction Facts Problems Write a word problem for each number sentence. Show how you would solve each problem. A. 6 + 9 = B. 15 − 7 =	Encourage students to share their strategies and explain how they solved the problems. A. 15 B. 8
20D Double the Number Double each of the following numbers. A. 6 B. 7 C. 9 D. 29 E. 62 F. 99 G. 73 H. 28 I. 14	 Encourage students to share their strategies. A. 12 B. 14 C. 18 D. 58 E. 124 F. 198 G. 146 H. 56 I. 28

20F **Math Facts and Families**

Solve the following problems. Then write the related facts in the same fact family.

A. $8 + 5 =$ _____

_____

_____

_____

B. $9 - 4 =$ _____

_____

_____

_____

C. $9 + 8 =$ _____

_____

_____

_____

D. $11 - 7 =$ _____

_____

_____

_____

E. $8 + 3 =$ _____

_____

_____

_____

F. $14 - 8 =$ _____

_____

_____

_____

A. $8 + 5 = 13$
$5 + 8 = 13$
$13 - 5 = 8$
$13 - 8 = 5$

B. $9 - 4 = 5$
$9 - 5 = 4$
$5 + 4 = 9$
$4 + 5 = 9$

C. $9 + 8 = 17$
$8 + 9 = 17$
$17 - 8 = 9$
$17 - 9 = 8$

D. $11 - 7 = 4$
$11 - 4 = 7$
$4 + 7 = 11$
$7 + 4 = 11$

E. $8 + 3 = 11$
$3 + 8 = 11$
$11 - 3 = 8$
$11 - 8 = 3$

F. $14 - 8 = 6$
$14 - 6 = 8$
$6 + 8 = 14$
$8 + 6 = 14$

Addition and Subtraction Math Facts Inventory

Take the inventory test your teacher will give. First, answer the questions you know well. Then go back to the questions you skipped. Answer the rest of the questions using strategies you learned.

This inventory test is located on the following page. The test combines both addition and subtraction facts. One fact problem is included from each of the fact families in Groups A–G, except facts with 0 and 1. However, a few fact problems with 0s and 1s are included. Most likely, if a student knows one fact in a fact family, he or she knows the other three facts in that family. For extra practice, students can write the other three related facts.

We do not recommend giving this test as a timed test. Your classroom schedule, however, may dictate that you limit the amount of time available. If this is the case, allow students who need extra time to change to a different colored pencil and finish as much of the test as they can.

Addition and Subtraction
Math Facts Inventory

1. $3 + 3 =$ **2.** $3 - 2 =$ **3.** $4 + 8 =$ **4.** $10 + 3 =$

5. $4 + 2 =$ **6.** $11 - 7 =$ **7.** $11 - 9 =$ **8.** $7 + 3 =$

9. $10 + 4 =$ **10.** $18 - 8 =$ **11.** $8 - 4 =$ **12.** $5 + 1 =$

13. $12 - 5 =$ **14.** $5 + 6 =$ **15.** $9 + 7 =$ **16.** $15 - 5 =$

17. $8 - 5 =$ **18.** $10 - 8 =$ **19.** $9 + 5 =$ **20.** $3 + 6 =$

21. $11 - 3 =$ **22.** $13 - 8 =$ **23.** $7 - 7 =$ **24.** $5 + 2 =$

25. 5 + 5 =   **26.** 5 − 3 =   **27.** 9 + 4 =   **28.** 7 + 6 =

29. 15 − 7 =   **30.** 9 − 2 =   **31.** 6 + 0 =   **32.** 9 + 8 =

33. 16 − 8 =   **34.** 3 − 0 =   **35.** 12 − 6 =   **36.** 9 + 9 =

37. 16 − 10 =   **38.** 12 − 9 =   **39.** 12 − 10 =   **40.** 10 − 4 =

41. 8 − 1 =   **42.** 2 + 2 =   **43.** 7 + 7 =   **44.** 15 − 9 =

45. 9 − 4 =   **46.** 10 + 7 =   **47.** 8 + 6 =   **48.** 2 + 6 =

49. 9 + 10 =   **50.** 7 − 3 =

This section includes the addition and subtraction *Triangle Flash Cards* for Groups A–G. See the Math Facts Calendar in Section 4 for when to use each group of *Triangle Flash Cards*.

Each card represents all four facts in a fact family. For example, $2 + 3 = 5$, $3 + 2 = 5$, $5 - 3 = 2$, $5 - 2 = 3$. When students are practicing the addition facts, remind them of the turn-around facts. If they know $3 + 2 = 5$, then they also know $2 + 3 = 5$.

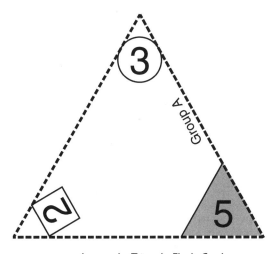

A sample *Triangle Flash Card*

When students are practicing the subtraction facts, they can go through the cards twice, once by covering the number in the square and once by covering the number in the circle. Alternatively, students can go through the cards once and then give the remaining subtraction fact in the fact family.

Triangle Flash Cards

Addition Practice

With a partner, use your *Triangle Flash Cards* to practice the addition or subtraction facts. If you are practicing addition, one partner covers the corner containing the highest number. This number will be the answer to an addition problem. The second person adds the two uncovered numbers.

$9 + 4 = ?$

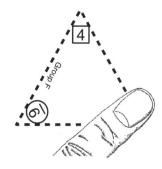

Sorting the Flash Cards

Separate the used cards into three piles: those facts you know and can answer quickly, those you can figure out with a strategy, and those you need to learn. Practice the last two piles again and then make a list of the facts you need to practice at home for homework.

Discuss how you can figure out facts you don't recall at once. Share your strategies with your partner.

Subtraction Practice

If you are practicing subtraction, cover the corner with the square. Subtract the uncovered numbers. Then go through the cards again, this time covering the number in the circle.

$13 - 9 = ?$

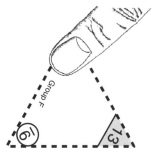

Triangle Flash Cards:
Group A

1. Cut out the flash cards.

2. Work with a partner. To practice an addition fact, cover the corner with the highest number. (It is shaded.) Add the two uncovered numbers.

3. Divide the cards into three piles: those facts you know and can answer quickly, those you can figure out, and those you need to learn.

4. Practice the last two piles again. Then make a list of the facts you need to practice.

5. To practice a subtraction fact, cover the corner with the square. Subtract the uncovered numbers. Then go through the cards again, this time covering the number in the circle.

6. Repeat the directions in 3 and 4 above each time you go through the cards.

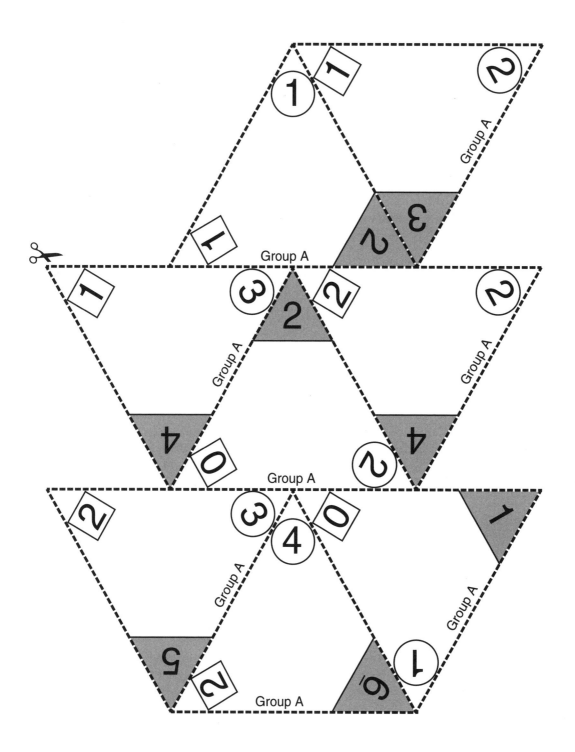

Triangle Flash Cards:
Group B

1. Cut out the flash cards.

2. Work with a partner. To practice an addition fact, cover the corner with the highest number. (It is shaded.) Add the two uncovered numbers.

3. Divide the cards into three piles: those facts you know and can answer quickly, those you can figure out, and those you need to learn.

4. Practice the last two piles again. Then make a list of the facts you need to practice.

5. To practice a subtraction fact, cover the corner with the square. Subtract the uncovered numbers. Then go through the cards again, this time covering the number in the circle.

6. Repeat the directions in 3 and 4 above each time you go through the cards.

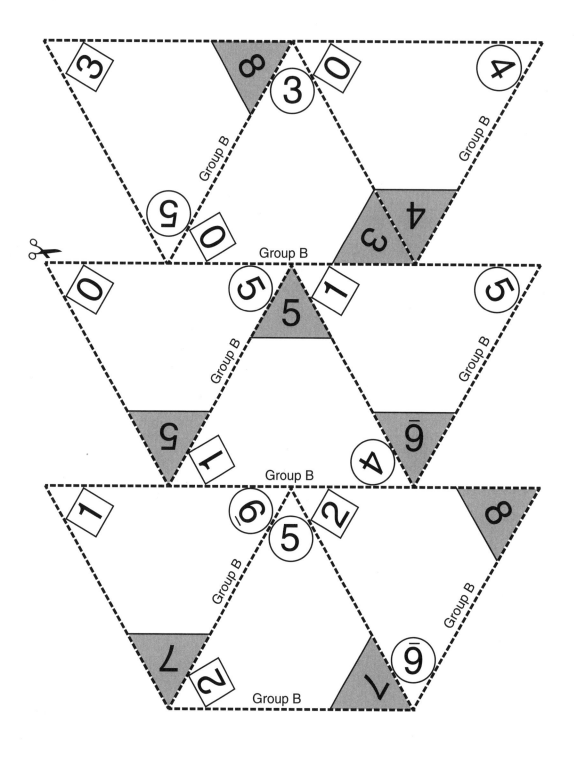

Group B

Group B

Group B

Group B

Group B

Group B

Group B

Group B

Triangle Flash Cards: Group C

1. Cut out the flash cards.

2. Work with a partner. To practice an addition fact, cover the corner with the highest number. (It is shaded.) Add the two uncovered numbers.

3. Divide the cards into three piles: those facts you know and can answer quickly, those you can figure out, and those you need to learn.

4. Practice the last two piles again. Then make a list of the facts you need to practice.

5. To practice a subtraction fact, cover the corner with the square. Subtract the uncovered numbers. Then go through the cards again, this time covering the number in the circle.

6. Repeat the directions in 3 and 4 above each time you go through the cards.

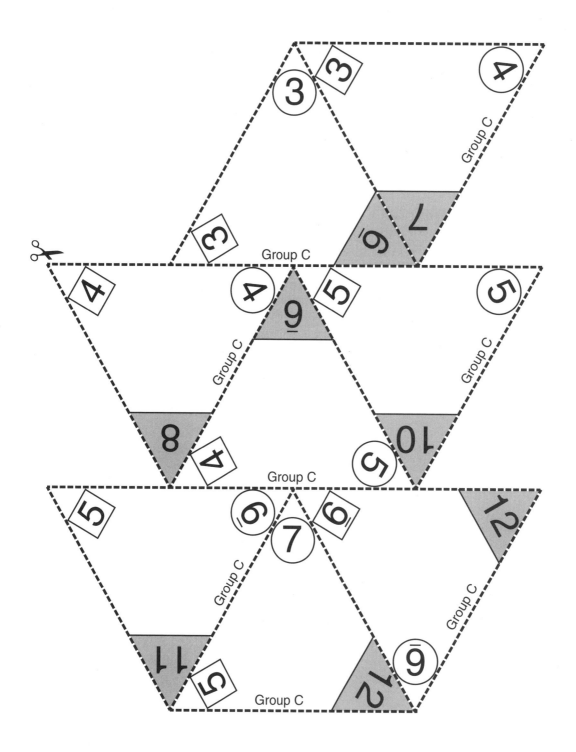

Copyright © Kendall/Hunt Publishing Company

Triangle Flash Cards: Group D

1. Cut out the flash cards.

2. Work with a partner. To practice an addition fact, cover the corner with the highest number. (It is shaded.) Add the two uncovered numbers.

3. Divide the cards into three piles: those facts you know and can answer quickly, those you can figure out, and those you need to learn.

4. Practice the last two piles again. Then make a list of the facts you need to practice.

5. To practice a subtraction fact, cover the corner with the square. Subtract the uncovered numbers. Then go through the cards again, this time covering the number in the circle.

6. Repeat the directions in 3 and 4 above each time you go through the cards.

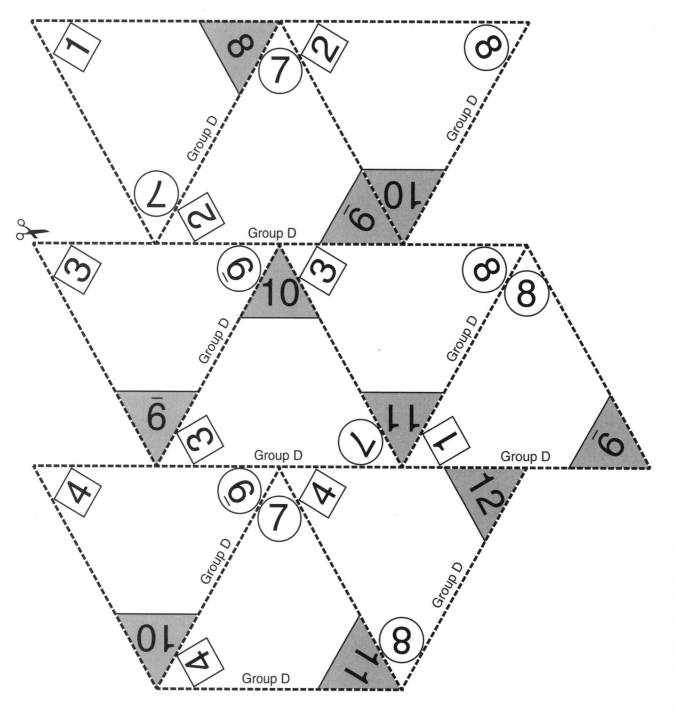

Group D

Group D

Group D

Group D

Group D

Group D

Group D

Group D

Triangle Flash Cards: Group E

1. Cut out the flash cards.

2. Work with a partner. To practice an addition fact, cover the corner with the highest number. (It is shaded.) Add the two uncovered numbers.

3. Divide the cards into three piles: those facts you know and can answer quickly, those you can figure out, and those you need to learn.

4. Practice the last two piles again. Then make a list of the facts you need to practice.

5. To practice a subtraction fact, cover the corner with the square. Subtract the uncovered numbers. Then go through the cards again, this time covering the number in the circle.

6. Repeat the directions in 3 and 4 above each time you go through the cards.

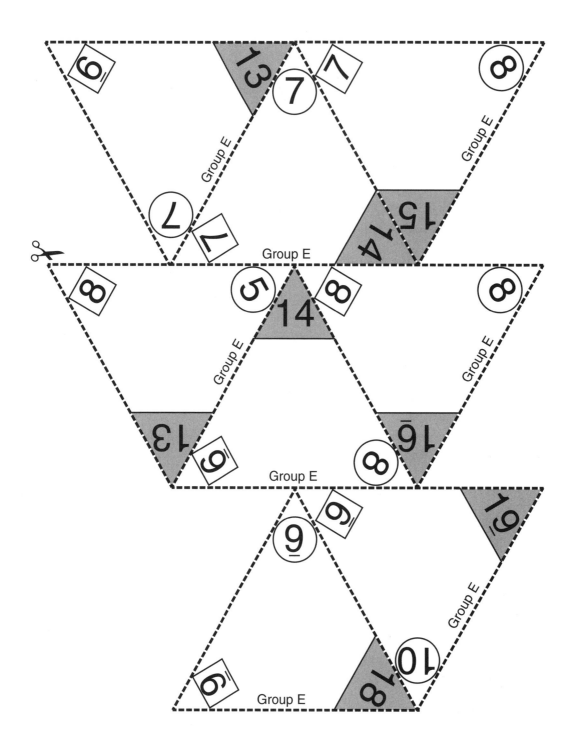

Group E

Triangle Flash Cards:
Group F

1. Cut out the flash cards.

2. Work with a partner. To practice an addition fact, cover the corner with the highest number. (It is shaded.) Add the two uncovered numbers.

3. Divide the cards into three piles: those facts you know and can answer quickly, those you can figure out, and those you need to learn.

4. Practice the last two piles again. Then make a list of the facts you need to practice.

5. To practice a subtraction fact, cover the corner with the square. Subtract the uncovered numbers. Then go through the cards again, this time covering the number in the circle.

6. Repeat the directions in 3 and 4 above each time you go through the cards.

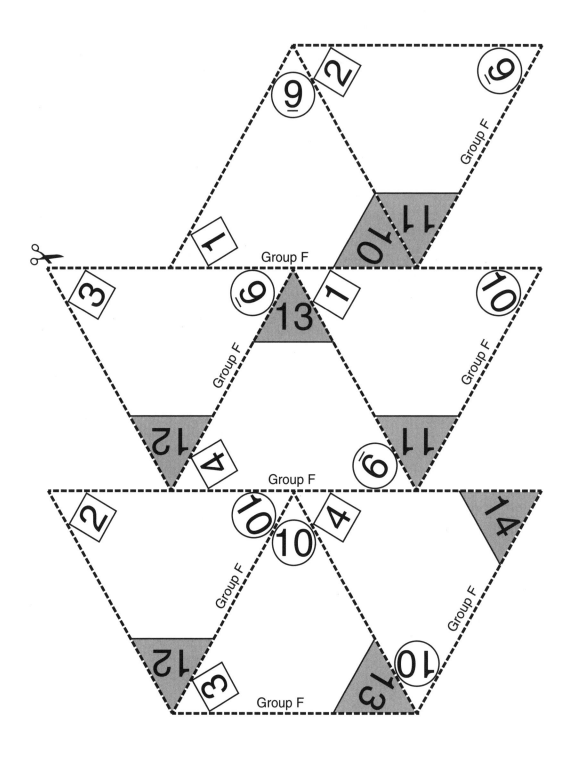

Triangle Flash Cards:
Group G

1. Cut out the flash cards.

2. Work with a partner. To practice an addition fact, cover the corner with the highest number. (It is shaded.) Add the two uncovered numbers.

3. Divide the cards into three piles: those facts you know and can answer quickly, those you can figure out, and those you need to learn.

4. Practice the last two piles again. Then make a list of the facts you need to practice.

5. To practice a subtraction fact, cover the corner with the square. Subtract the uncovered numbers. Then go through the cards again, this time covering the number in the circle.

6. Repeat the directions in 3 and 4 above each time you go through the cards.

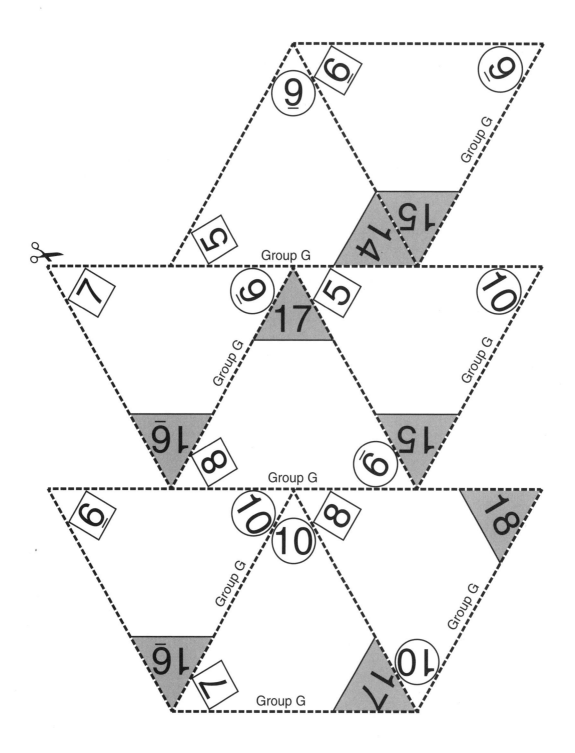